CHANGE A MAN

PROJECT

CHANGE A MAN
PROJECT

Library of Congress Cataloging-in-Publication Data
Robinson, Devin
YA: fiction / Devin Robinson
ISBN: 978-0-9828550-3-4
Cover Design by: Devin Robinson
Illustration by: Damian Flores

The paper used in this publication meets the minimum requirements of the America National Standard for Information Sciences—Permanence of Paper for Printed Library Materials, ANSIZ39.48-1984.

Contents

Introduction:

CHANCE 2 CHANGE
By Doe

Now you're praying for another shot
Her leaving you,
Has led you to the bar paying for another shot
She mentioned it before,
But didn't know whether to believe it or not
Disgusted with birthdays and anniversaries that I often forgot

My addiction to money got stronger than that smile I used to be a
fiend for
Now no more star gazing and walking hand in hand along the
seashore

Love is a crazy journey,
Roadblocks you're going to run into
But constant reminders are signs he ain't trying
He'll make the necessary changes if he wants you

At one point, the risk of losing you was a faint thought in my head
Complacency somehow got the best of me, and now it's
December in my bed

I gave her cold shoulders,
So now I'm taking cold showers!
She didn't want rose gold,
Just a dozen white flowers!
And a random text saying how much you thinking bout her,
But she couldn't fight for my heart no more,
So she threw in her towel

Right after she asked me would I rather make cash or make love?
My hesitation confirmed her answer...she's in love with a thug

So it's best to leave me now than to wait and do it later
Because if you give me another chance to change, you might

regret it later

You know that I can't find a job, and you know what i just got out c
jail for
You accepted me with nothing, told me don't worry about nothing
So I felt like "what I gotta change for?"

A man gonna do what you let him do,
He can't cross it if you never put a line
When the ball is in your court,
YOU call out the rules!
So don't blame him for wasting your time

Cause when it all hits the fan,
You find out who's the real man
Pressure will make little boys leave quick!
So demand your change,
A real man will come your way
And change at the very first chance he get...

Written by a former convict, college dropout and drug dealer.
Now an amazing father of two, proud man of God and becoming
the man he knows...he can be. It didn't take a woman to change
him, just knowing life with his daughters is worth more than money
can ever account for. This poem brings to light two messages you'll
find later in this book; how "bad boys" think and how that relates to
changing any man. Enjoy your journey, this is the introduction.

Chapter 1:
How God Made Me a Hypocrite

A man will string you along as long as you allow him to. You have a choice in being a "life" girlfriend or wife. -Egypt

Chapter 1:
How God Made Me A Hypocrite

Understand one thing, this idea isn't mine. If someone forcefully placed a knife to my face, daring to slice my flesh...I would still deny the assumption that women could change men. Why? When this disgusting topic of changing a man arises, it's always directed towards a woman upgrading the most broken, useless and hapless man. It's as if women aim only to waste their time; never giving men who could love them the way they deserve to be loved a chance. Rather than fixing the tires of a new Bentley, she'd rather donate hours of non-redemptive labor on remodeling a 94' Honda Civic. Who could convince me of urging my sisters to support this poisonous idea? Only God could. But why?

As the seemingly biggest rival against the changing of a man, I seemed much like Saul in the Holy Bible. He was definitely anti-Christian but God used him to inspire the world about Jesus Christ. Sometimes your enemy can be your greatest sponsor. I was that enemy. The sheer level of venom I spat regarding this issue was unbelievable. Verbally demolishing women via online message boards when this filthy idea would slick pass my screen. Others began to follow my belief system regarding this. My voice was an expeller against any hope in regards to this subject. God knew if I spoke people would listen. Then He spoke and I listened.

One day while in church, my princess and I intently indulged in the sermon. Something was off. My mind escaped the message. I left the moment and began to feel my mind massage the question of "why men need to be changed?" It was maybe due to the lack of young male presence in the church. Why were young men absent? Did we only attend church after 30? Where were we? What was keeping us away? A better inquiry would be...who could bring us back?

"Only God can change men" is the common note given when I speak about this book. Well, who will lead him there? Jesus came as a man to lead men to God. He didn't do it as a goat, monkey or leopard, but a man. In Genesis, you read that out of God's need for man to have a comparable helper He created woman. He created woman for the mission of helping a man. Not to be his footstool, but helper. The woman is the only key to bringing the man back to God. We are lost without woman. We chase woman. We love woman. If we must travel through

Him to get to woman, we will. This was what God was pushing me to do front of my near 5,000 followers, I became a believer.

Many thought it was a joke, fluke or jive to bait women. Baiting them into believing men can't be changed. It was humbling to contrad myself for no reward. Many know me as a consistent man of my word. Lying is what weak men do. Being obedient is what I did. Meekness isn't weakness and thus is what was necessary for me to bring myself to this writing. I was key to inspiring this message.

When a man inspires women to inspire men it weighs heavier than c woman inspiring women to inspire men. Why? You don't really see many men inspiring women in this day and age. Yet, men are to be co-inspirers in the lives of women. However, if boys occupy a woman's time, she will live in one way-inspiration, only inspiring him. Women deserve men, not boys.

Men have a sense of faith. Boys aren't in search of that sense. Men want to build women into better beings. Boys would rather a free ride while corrupting a woman's integrity. As I tend to say, "If a broke man car afford your self-esteem, he will buy it at a discount." Many of our women are entertaining boys who are discouraged at becoming men. These boy aren't creating love but sucking the love out of women and replacing it with lust, betrayal or depression.

This book is written to empower the reader. I want you to understand no woman needs a man to validate herself as a woman. However, it would be glorious for her to share her heart, love and mind with someone who deserves, earns and accepts it. If she can inspire him to bite the apple of righteousness, care and forgiveness, he will bite. Eve changed the world within a day. After this read, you will have some of her formula.

A man will be only what he's encouraged to be. When no one attends his basketball games, he may not even show up. However, if the benches are sparsely occupied with female spectators screaming his name, he knows there's hope in his actions. He will train, work harder and do more just to obtain that "high" of female attention.

Women have the power to better us. It is through their motivation, direction and sacrifice that men can finally overtake the church. Not in authority, but attendance. They will get off the streets, out of the jails and into colleges. Maybe they all won't become graduates but at least they won't continue to fail in the masses. Women are our saving grace. The

4

race we've abused, misused and refused to love properly, but stays. If these brothers can learn to love them right, get to God and become better men, we will win as a human race.

If you don't believe a woman can change a man then ask yourself this...if not women*...then who? If you can't answer, then allow this solution to last until you find a better route.

This method is based on human behavior. I picked heterosexual female and male interaction as the majority basis for the book yet it's not denying those of other sexual preferences success while using this technique.

Chapter 2:
Who And What Changed Me?

Chapter 2:
Who And What Changed Me?

Sex, lies, anger, fame and headaches spurred change in me. Little did I know it was just God finding a way to make me a better me. This is the story of who and what changed me.

An HIV-positive love interest, a Native American princess, a feminist lesbian, an African model, a Haitian future doctor and a confused woman who used sex as the admission to her heart are the 6 women who changed me. While I won't disclose each relationship and how intimate we were, I'll begin to talk about the "safe" stories.

She leapt off a plane from freezing Minnesota to embrace my warm, open Florida arms. We engaged in the most schizophrenic time in my life. Prior to her arrival, I could promise you I adored this young woman beyond belief. The moment she ended the initial embrace...I wanted her to leave. It was then when I realized I wasn't mentally ready to love. This was a horrible time in my life. I was 22, received national attention from exposure from MTV and just answered the definitive internal inquisition, "What do you want to become?" This new feeling and uncertainty of how to deal with it caused anger.

This Native American woman has a heart of gold. She is currently married, happy and a blessing to her husband as he is to her. While she was in my life, I was harsh, avoidant and unaffectionate to her. Oddly, she changed me by my actions. Sometimes men hurt women who don't deserve to be hurt. I can't blame my youth, it was just stupidity. When a man damages a woman, excuses should be the last to escape his lips. She was a sacrifice. From her, I learned to handle my anger differently. I had **faith** in being a better person from this situation. Amazingly, this was my thought process while going through it. Just goes to show many men know they are wrong but refuse to defeat the burdensome tick of wrongdoing.

Most recently I apologized to this woman. Another action I knew to do but waited too long to accomplish. It was a passionate message that was years in the making. She accepted my apology and healed me in the process. After her, I ran into other scenarios when being dismissive of a woman's feelings benefited me.

Enter the future doctor from South Florida. She was one of few women to gain my sister's approval. Just to give you an idea of how rare

9

this is I've only had three women in 10 years to be approved by my sister. Her word ruled since the death of my mother. She became the matriarch of my family. Although young, her judgment is law. Even prophetic with analysis of ladies I entertained. All women she deemed "fishy"...were fish and deserved the diagnosis. This young lady, who she approved of, was in my heart in ways I didn't dream. However, I was new to "fame" and the intense level of attention associated with it. From such a poor reasoning of "I'm new to fame", I was very angry at times. Sometimes it was directed towards her. She didn't deserve it. When it was time to move the relationship forward, she didn't follow. I learned that no one deserves to be your outlet for confusion. She helped teach me such. Her **environmental control** was that only positivity reigned. My negativity caused my departure. Something I would execute later on.

Lesbians are typically women who only date women. This lesbian was a lesbian who dated women and...me. I became the only man she believed inspired her. I was "different". So was she. I never met a more confused, deranged and schizophrenic woman in my life. She taught me about loving myself enough not to deal with someone's inability to love themselves. She was very abusive. Abusive in ways I've never before seen It wasn't physical, verbal or spiritual, just mental. Her **penalty** for my not desiring sex was barking. She would yell, scream and aggravate me until I submitted. It was teaching. My **prize** for submitting was sex, food and no aggravation. Never in my life was I in fear of not having sex with a woman It wasn't fear of being beaten, just enduring another argument. I began to lose hair and to a young man, hair is a vanity much loved. Before her, I saw what happens when someone's word doesn't meet their actions. She wanted to be a good person, but her movements didn't match, much like the person who inspired my first book. Let's call her, the Conniving Convenient Convincing Conference Liar.

We had sex at a convention, agreed to keep it a secret and seemingly before I could leave the room...everyone knew we had sex. The whispers only grew when we left the conference and returned to campus. My instinct was to approach her about these rumors. It was determined the origin of such gossip is unknown so it's best to deny. I obliged only to find out she was the one telling the story. She didn't practice what she preached. My first two years of college were ruined courtesy of a woman lying about what was agreed upon. She didn't speak with **conviction.** She only spoke what would enable her to keep this charade living. I learned that if you practice what you preach, you could live in dignity. Never telling other men about my love life was a word I lived in with **conviction.** She had no honor; only lied with **conviction** and that helped me see such.

Although I experienced much painstaking stressful semesters, this led many who believed in my integrity to follow me thus creating the organization AIDS Awareness Poets Inc. I own this day. Without them, I wouldn't be blessed to bless many people with information about HIV, relationships and love. When you see me, hear my words or performances, it's all about the same matter. When I began to help people with HIV, it was important because many needed another voice in the weakening war. Since 03', I've been loud. I will fight until the battle is over courtesy of learning that **conviction** in your word is worth more than flexibility with it.

These women helped bring about my change. I became a better man by their teaching. Why I paid attention to these things instead of living in the moment is gray to me. My pain will now lead you to being a better person because this book can be used on men...and women. I just believe men need the most help.

For reasons which will follow later in this writing, bad boys have it easy. I've grown exhausted with being good and running into ruined women, as many other self-proclaimed good men have. Boys who couldn't love them have broken these women. Broken by waiting for them to reach a potential they never met. Broken by babysitting an adult. Adding to such, when you were what they desired, these women perceived you as "too good to be true." This sad belief, a lack of patience and poor standards of many women lead to my torment.

Seeing women give up and accept whoever is available only to become destroyed helped spur my interest in writing this. No good man feels happy about working hard only to receive a bad boy's straps especially when that bad boy didn't work for it.

Many women are victims of wasting time with a man who could never become what they need. These are the same women who pray for a good man only to lose patience and date a bad boy who isn't on their level.
 This book is aimed to teach about *who* we entertain and understanding ways to better them. Strong emphasis is on who we date. In my finding, this maniacal trend of dating boys instead of men is hurting our women. The old adage, "Patience is a virtue" will help in this read.

Society has taught women an ugly form of patience. Waiting until exhausted only to accept what will tarnish, not build. Patience is a verb. It's an action word. Patience is something you do, not merely waiting but actively preparing for a blessing.

When you pray for a good man, you don't just sit, twiddle your thumbs and hope he pops into your home. It's similar to baking a turkey. While the turkey is in the oven, you arrange the other compliments, set the table, organize the condiments, clean up and ready yourself for the meal. When the turkey is done, you are able to eat it without wasting time on setting the table, arranging the cranberry sauce and other compliments to this dish. If you didn't prepare while you were waiting, the turkey would become cold, dry or not as optimal once you were done with the preparations.

When being patient for a man, it's important to know staying healthy, God-fearing and mindful of your actions are "cooking" directions as God prepares your man. If you rush the process, you might desire to find something that you can eat faster. It won't be as good as turkey, probably unhealthy and cheap. Your impatience is sure to end in sickness, bitterness and doubt of God's ability to answer prayers. Women in the Holy Bible waited for years despite what was told to them. They succeeded because of patience. This was a startling find as I grew.

Watching women I knew lowering their standards at the sight of reaching past childbearing age seemed odd how they chased available, temporary attention but not investment. Thus, I wanted to make a clear difference between men who will invest versus boys who would make a donation.

Good men invest time into a woman. Bad boys donate time to women. An investment is something worthwhile. When you invest, you typically only invest what you have in limited supply to gain a high return on investment. A donation is charity. You only donate out of your plenty. You never donate your last or dare to. I thought if women could understand this, the benefits of patience and my struggle, they would begin to understand why changing a man is beneficial.

This book is my testimony, research and thoughts. What changed me? Pain and understanding. Who changed me? Experience, Pain and Understanding. What will change him? My pain, understanding, experience, your love and this teaching. Who you are and what you do plays the biggest part in the effectiveness of this technique.

None of this will matter, none of your effort will produce fruit, none of the change will be possible if you fit the description of the following chapter.

Chapter 3:
Who Should Not Read This Book?

**If you don't believe in the standards you set...
nor will he. ~ Egypt**

Chapter 3:
Who Should Not Read This Book?

Anyone can become a millionaire but not everyone will become a millionaire. What separates the millionaires from the almost millionaires is dedication to an ambitious assignment. This book isn't designed to become a be-all for any woman. No math book can make you an expert mathematician but the book, alongside zeal and consistency can take you from student to professor. There are a few who will be better off using this book as fun reading, decoration or gift to a friend who doesn't fit the below characters. Until you make this book your voice, it is just a silent leashed image of possibilities. Use this, if you can and become one of the many who will…change him.

Women who refuse to believe they too were created in God's image.

In Genesis, God created man and woman on the 6th day. It was in His image that He created woman. Now, He only created woman because He wanted man to have a "comparable helper". That's what a woman is: A man's helper who shares the image of God and is similar to man. Nothing in that represents inferiority. A woman is able to help man become a better man not because of this book but because God placed women here to help us. He could have placed goats, monkeys and chickens to be our comparable helpers but instead, He took the woman from the rib (womb) of man to make him a helper, hence (wo)man. If you don't believe you are here to help us, then you won't be able to. A teacher who believes she can't teach her students…won't. Believe you can and you will.

Women who notoriously date men they shouldn't.

Yes, this book can change any man but the man must desire the woman in order to change. Women who date deadbeat men are typically dating men who consider the woman as an option, not a priority. Most deadbeat men or rebellious men have noted, as you will read, the grand prize in not submitting to meeting their full potential. Thus, the process of changing him will take much longer. Women who date men they shouldn't typically aren't built with enough self-control to stick with their demands. In the long run, if she sticks to her guns, she will win but odds are, if she isn't a priority, lacks persistence and conviction, she'll just lose the battle of changing him.

Women who are mistresses, booty calls or one-night stands.

As stated above, in order for this book to work, a man has to deem you, "a priority." If you are just someone he's sleeping or cheating with, you aren't important enough for him to change. Think about it, if he can have sex with you and there is no initial demand of titles, then why change? A man has to desire your heart for this to be effective. You have to be a priority beyond the momentary sexual urge. If you are not important after sex, you were never important to begin with. This book will just be a reminder of what you can do to your boyfriend, fiancé or husband.

Women who won't change but want him to change

As career coach, Lynne Guillaume, states, "If you aren't willing to change into what you're asking him to change into, then it's a waste of time." In essence, it's similar to asking him to eat better while you eat worse or unhealthy altogether. Many times we want to ask our mates to halt actions without checking ourselves prior to such demands. In the Holy Bible it states: "Why do you look at the speck of sawdust in your brother's eye and pay no attention to the plank in your own eye?" It's the same conclusion. Change yourself before you change him. If you want him to stop smoking, be willing to stop yourself or any other negative attribute he may detail. In order to grow together, both must change together or fail together. He can't be the only one who needs changing. No one is without flaw.

Remember, this isn't a man-bashing book. The man isn't the subject in this book. The construction of a healthy relationship is the subject.

In the end, if you don't fit any of the above cast members, make sure you are ready to exert the energy and your partner is worth the energy.

Chapter 4:
Is He Even Worth The Energy?

If you don't demand progression, you're silently
telling him, "It's okay to stay where we are"
~ Egypt

Chapter 4:
Is He Even Worth The Energy?

What more could accompany this chapter besides the title? This is one question women must often ask themselves while entertaining a troubling man. While you are preparing to read the FEP-C® formula, understanding this question will save you time and energy.

For women who answer the question in an affirmative answer, then they will enjoy this read while creating cute custom ways of changing their man. When you know they are worth the energy, these directions aren't cumbersome. It's very reminiscent of gaining a degree. From the onset, you're reminded it may cost you tens of thousands of dollars and 4+years. Some look at the time, money and effort only to find refuge in refusing. Others will see this as an investment into something worthwhile. Many who obtain a degree can attest to finally reaping what they've sown. Although for some, even though the student loans may inspire a little bitterness when time passes, it only encourages happiness as they see the fruit in their durability. If your mate isn't something you can truly see as a lifelong investment, save this book for a new partner, donate it to a friend in the meantime and reevaluate your standards for suitable mates. It may be them...or you.

Women who say, "No, he isn't worth the energy" should delve into why he was so blessed to be in their life in the first place. If he isn't worth it, what did he do that was so special to invigorate her acceptance? Maybe he lied, the truth is out and his value as a man has diminished. Maybe he was never worth it to begin with but she thought donating attention would jolt his desire to meet the potential she sees in him. Maybe he didn't meet his potential and she's tired of wasting irretrievable youth on this man. Endless reasons can exist but none matter. If she isn't up to enduring more, then this book won't help her. It takes her desire and his desire to create success in this book. If she doesn't desire him and he doesn't desire to change for her, then this book is only an interesting read for the "what if I was dating a man who was worth the energy?"

If a man isn't worth your tailoring a campaign to halt his wrongdoing or inspiring him to do what he knows is right, bolt for the door. Remember, answer truthfully and you will own a better understanding of what it takes to change him...because it starts with you.

Chapter 5:
Desire Of Wrongdoing
Meets
Desire To Do Right

Chapter 5:
Desire Of Wrongdoing
Meets
Desire To Do Right.

These two powerful questions may lead to two painful answers: Does he know what he's doing is wrong? If so, does he desire to change such behavior? Many men have been so successful at being horrible men that they've come to see their actions as, "good". Even some truly good men have oddly negative or unfavorable attributes but are innocent to knowing the injuries they cause their mates. Thus, in the realms of altering such a mindset or personal movement, he's lost as to the internal inquiry, "What am I doing wrong?"

This isn't a hard hurdle to leap. The agony of never asking this question may cause inevitable stressful battles and many mini-momentary breakups. Also, prepare for the seemingly naïve response he may riddle out of his mouth. The overwhelmingly common, "It's how I was raised", "I don't know any other way to be" or the incomparable "This is who I am" are responses most women should know already. They may appear to be ignorant, poor or putrid excuses yet sadly, may show you how innocent being a bad man is.

First, she must assess if he is aware of his negative actions. For instance: If he constantly puts her down with harsh words, yet she never tells him such hurt or if she does, he casts her off as, "being too sensitive", then she has an issue. It is here where she must alert him of the true pain his actions are causing. No matter if she's being too sensitive or not, the world is full of demeaning, evil and damaging words for/images of women. When she's home, she should not have to deal with it from her mate.

Second, she must ask, "Do you want to make me happy by refraining from calling me names?" This is an opportunity for her to gauge if her battle will take minutes or months. If he says, "You know love, yes, I will stop" then bravo and buy a watch to peer at how long it takes him to change. If he utters, "This is me, this is who I am. I won't change for anyone." Then, buy a calendar because you're going to be here a while.

Lastly, whatever the circumstance, the woman must realize her life isn't about accepting pain in exchange for potential pleasure. What you accept now will be what you accept later. Later doesn't always guarantee his verbal abuse will lighten. As we age, grow and learn from partner, we begin to specialize in words that hurt. Cut it at the roots and let them know.

When you assess if he's aware of his wrongdoing and is willing to do right, you're on your way to a healthy end to a negative action.

From here, you are getting prepared to endure the FEP-C ® formula to curve his behavior. Another hurdle will be breaking down his excuses or reasons to identify an avenue to begin.

Chapter 6:
Excuse v. Reason. Round 1

Excuse V. Reason. Round 1

Excuses are tools of the incompetent used to build monuments of nothing and those who specialize in them seldom do well in anything in life except…excuses -Unknown.

Prior to engaging the journey of this very interesting and intrinsic battle, you must first be wired with proper ammunition. A man will use this word like a gun with unlimited bullets. Your goal is to limit his ammo and render his weapon useless. His scapegoat of choice is called…excuses. Yet, not only the usage, he will clearly speak in a manner which leads you to believe his "overwhelming" excuses aren't preventable or able to be overcome. You will be trapped in the inner conflict of deciding if his paralyzing excuses are in fact true reasons. However, the contrast between the two is beyond evident and completely discriminatory.

The difference between reasons and excuses is simple. Reasons are irrefutable facts. Ex: "I can't walk because my legs are amputated." Excuses are surmountable and extremely debatable reasons one gives another or themselves to avoid doing something. Ex: "I can't walk because, it's hot outside and I may sweat too much." Find out which he's giving first and conquer the issue second. Now that you're supplied with the healing shield to deflect the first wave of his words, the rest of your armory is below.

Man, in some respects, is a synonym for "excuse donator". Many men are pleasantly afforded an unlimited amount of excuse tickets to avoid the complexity of paying the…truth and responsibility price. Oddly, women are the owners of these opportunities and thus the bearers of such tickets. Sadly, women are the ones hurt most by the usage of excuses. If you accept a man's excuse, he'll give you more. It's nothing short of common sense. In reality, if you could gain a degree by simply informing your professors, "You should allow me to succeed because my past was horrible", would you really study, read or work diligently towards your specialty?

When conquering excuses in your relationship, please be mindful of these facts:

1. *"Fear breeds excuses"*-Pastor Reggie Royal of Lifeline Church in Chicago, Illinois.

2. You are the sum total of your past, including yesterday but not the victim of it.

3. Either learn from your past or lose because of it.

Let's begin to divide and conquer each of these facts to add courage where there may have been despair regarding your attempts of *Changing Him.*

"Fear Breeds Excuses"

Most people, not only men, are fearful of change. We don't welcome it with open arms or a steady heart. We've been this way since youth. There was a time when you weren't ready to use a toilet, yet you defeated your fears and accomplished a task you barely think of as challenging today. No matter the challenge, it's only the initial thought, decision and action needed to beat any fear. Ex: When do you think roller coasters are most "scary"? Unbelievably it's not while on the coaster, but the walk up to the line, followed by the moment before you step on. Oddly once on, you've already begun to lose "fear" of this as you change from a spectator to rider. Why so? Because you unconsciously said to yourself, "I can do this".

Note, when using this book's ideas on excuses, be mindful of why we fear change. As long as you know why we fear changing of anything, it will affect your approach. If knowing fear will inspire excuses, think of the roller coaster. What are the properties of this machine that inspire the rider to go from knocking out their initial desires of staying at home, on the ground or away…to riding it? It's the marketing and pressure. Are you properly marketing the reasons why they should change? Are you giving clear and sufficient reasons why their excuse isn't efficient enough to warrant missing such a fun ride? A roller coaster is typically 100-1000 times larger than the rider yet we get on. In the same sense, you can make taking out the garbage, for example, a fun and exciting change. First, why should they? Ex: The house will smell so much better, we won't have to see pesky bugs and it makes me want to kiss your chest more seeing a man take out the garbage.

Although the example may live in reality, the point is made. When you desire to defeat one of his many excuses, first make what you're giving attractive. We only conquered the toilet because it seemed harmless and we received treats once we did so. Remember, at 1-3 years old, the toilet was the largest immovable roller coaster in the land. It was taller, bigger, and louder than you plus required our stepping outside the norm for completion. Apply the same to helping him win over the excuses

28

...e gives but never accept them. If your parents did, you would wear
Depends now instead of underwear.

You aren't a victim of your past

The most widely used and accepted excuses derive from a man's
past. For example: "I can't love you the way you deserve to be loved
because...I was never loved that way." Now, I understand, in regards to
the heart, empathy and care of a human's emotions, however, being
that this book isn't written to create smiles now but to ensure smiles in the
long-term future, I'm only being honest in my next statement.

You are the owner of your pain as long as you allow him usage of
old excuses. It's as simple as the above. Ironically, many already know the
dynamics which create the truth behind the statement. Yet, some women
are infected with an idea that, "His past can't be overcome" or the
infamous," I understand, baby" syndrome. It needs to end *now*!

Not having loving parents, growing up in the ghetto, hood or in
unfavorable surroundings, losing family to horrific circumstances, living in
multiple "fight or flight" situations or being abused are all disgustingly
traditional storylines of many men. What makes it something to smile
about is...many of these men rose to become more than their past and
are now called, President Barack Obama, Jesus Christ, King David,
Malcolm X, Job, Ancel Pratt III, Lucson Joseph...etc It's almost uncanny
how many successful and historic men exist with such terrifying pasts yet
they are written about on a daily basis. Men like Rev. Dr. Martin Luther King
Jr. even have their own holiday yet these men suffered pasts riddled with
quite well known feats. They didn't live as victims of the cards they were
dealt but rather, they went on to become masterful poker players despite
the layout. Your man is a king. He just may not know it or isn't living up to it
but he is. Every man has the capabilities to be more than they are.

Our past is easily overcome by desire, love and history. *"It takes a
good woman to bring out the best in a man. It takes a good man to bring
out the best in a woman."* -Honorable Louis Farrakhan. Does he desire to
be better than his past? Ask him. Sincerely, not condescendingly but ask,
"Do you want to overcome this?" I'm not asking you to say, "Can you
overcome this?" We know he can but asking if he wants to will expose a
deeper root to his ailment. If you're a good woman, one who loves,
supports and inspires, you will bring out the best in him. First, it starts with his
desire to live beyond his yesterday and use it to create a more awe
inspiring today. Knowing this question is coming from a lover and loving

heart helps with his honesty. If he betters himself, he will better you. i   a cycle.

Dear reader, understand many men are broken in this day and age. Yes, we are strong in appearance, physically beat women, verbally abuse them and some are charged with writing bills to minus rights of women but all are signs of fear and weakness. Why are they doing this? They know you are powerful enough to make us better. You must belie e When asking him this, know that it must be from the deepest crevice of your heart. Break the yoke of evil and intake the filling of goodness. This begins after you've learned if it's an excuse or reason.

When you've gained this answer take into account where this excuse was born. His past gives access to the birth of this pain/fear and a cure. If his upbringing was harsh and filled with more reasons to cry than to smile, that's okay. Learn his story then tell him yours. Give him comparable history to define why it won't bury his tomorrow. If your history isn't reflective of someone who went through pain to see pleasure, then research any of the men above and use a few other stories of men you know to bring the point home. Sometimes we like to think those who came before us were something beyond comparison, so we exclude them as "possible" yet we all know another person or story of someone who defied the odds and made something of themselves. If anything, you know my story. Use this knowledge as a tool to thwart his past and redirect his attention to bettering his today.

Learn from your past or lose from it

The American prison system is overpopulated with White, Asian, Hispanic and Black men, who had an evident chance to go to college, raise children, earn a living and become model citizens but somehow took an extreme left down "Incarceration Avenue". Men who share my story of poverty, loss and in-game decision-making are somewhat villains to incarcerated women and men or their lovers who believe, "They never had a chance". Unless they were one of the many unfortunates who were falsely accused, they were convicted as an adult. In addition, they had a TV, eyes or a radio. No matter what they watched or listened to, there was another land of opportunity but they made a decision to explore an alternate route and fell victim to their choice.

This isn't a finger pointing session, this is reality. I sold drugs, fought, pimped and was arrested on multiple occasions. If I had kept this mindset up after 18, I would be writing about myself as an institutional prisoner.

30

Why is this imperative to our written dialogue, you may ask? Well, many of those same men will exit those failed prison systems only to return to those walls with the excuse, "There wasn't any work for a convict and I had no choice but to commit a crime." They fell prey to a belief that their pasts are invincibly alluring and insurmountable, thus it's easier to stay a convict than to become a conqueror.

In essence, his past has full control of his present thoughts and behavior. He has an area of relief as to where he can assert his, "It can't be done" claim. He's fully aware that others have left imprisonment to become millionaires or legends, Don King, Paul (Acts 16:23) Jay –Z, Robert Downey Jr., and James Brown are examples. The prison rhetoric is only aimed to expose the reality of the mere fact that these men are still prisoners, not inmates in a physical building but of their minds.

As long as we believe it can't be done, we will live in that falsehood. This will keep him from being a "good man". Remember, a good man is what you deserve. What you accept is a different story. When you truly believe you deserve the best, you will wonder why he's allowed to use his past to hurt you and himself. He may not be a physical repeated convict, as stated, but he is mentally. Every time he uses what has happened as a reason to never improve, that's the sign of a repeat offender. From here, he's beating himself. You deserve better. You deserve the best. You deserve him moving beyond self-inflicted wounds to begin an arduous process of healing.

You can help him heal. He will do most of the work but you can lay the groundwork. The groundwork is: prayer, asking him about his past and giving him history of those with similar pasts. This may require research but if you plan on loving him forever, be prepared to do work. Understand his toil but never accept it as a reason. Show him why his inability to get beyond his past hurts him in addition to you. Lastly, give visual, mental or physical incentives as to why he should move on. Ex: Visual - display vacation photos of distant places you can visit once he's happy. Mental - express the level of intelligence he has and once coupled with action, how he can create things he's thought of or finish them. Physical - once he takes a step closer, give him a back, head or hand massage. Bare in mind, what you do for him, he has the example to do for you. Unless you're in existence with a man who is completely void of happiness, you'll receive some form of immediate pleasure for these actions.

Dear reader,

Don't be afraid to put fire on him. Nothing stays the same in fire. When you burn a napkin, it becomes ash. When you heat up water, it becomes mist or vapor. When dry skin meets sunlight it becomes wet ski due to perspiration or sun burnt. You can be his fire of change. You can ignite the fire that fuels the flame, which creates a new excuse-free mar When we live without excuses, we become a dangerous form of human A human with an interesting desire to prove ourselves, others and tomorrow wrong. We begin to live with an eager inner ignition waiting to meet a spark only to overcome any obstacle with unforgiving and undefeatable flames of change. A great legendary boxing trainer once said, "*A boy comes to me with a spark of interest, I feed the spark and it becomes a flame. I feed the flame and it becomes a fire. I feed the fire and it becomes a roaring blaze.*"-Cus D' Amato. You are that trainer, he your fighter and excuses are the opponent. When you walk into that ring all you will have is you and your fighter. The odds may be stacked again you. The gamblers may have counted your fighter out. Everyone with an opinion to give has already picked you and him to lose...by first round knockout! No matter their belief, no matter what they know, no matter how much an underdog, when you've understood what needs to be done to defeat "excuses", you're preparing for a historical upset; larger than Tyson vs. Douglas or David and Goliath.

Excuses dethrone most relationships. Both good and bad people suffer from this human behavioral trait. This is the fight. You can win. The bell is about to be rung. Please don't leave it in the judges' hands. Go for the knockout. You have the fire to encourage his victory over excuses an into change.

Chapter 7:
Are You Encouraging...
Or Aggravating?

Chapter 7:

Are You Encouraging... Or Aggravating?

This chapter, although brief will donate one of the most important lessons a person can learn. If you allow your mind to interpret any of the doctrine or teachings inside these pages, you'll note I'm not asking you to be only a "change agent" but more so a leader. Great leaders do many great things. The most notable is, inspire.

When you encourage someone to accomplish a task, it's typically something where you're pushing him or her to do better than they previously believed they could. It is here where you see that once "hole-in-the-wall" mom and popshop spring into a fortune 500 company. They may have only employed a hand full of people but with each one, they gave a reason to do better, tools to complete it, a verbal push in a desired direction, reward for meeting standard and reminder of why they should finish the feat. This is called, "encouragement." It's a fundamental necessity in leadership.

Think of the boss who only yells, reminds you of what you do wrong, never admits the times you do it right and consistently makes the work environment unhealthy with their attitude, energy and horrible leadership. That is someone who is more so an aggravator than leader. Aggravating someone isn't a great form of leadership in any group. It's one of the prime ways to lose employees and in this case a mate. The rule of thumb in differentiating between encouragement and aggravation is defining how you feel after you've committed the act.

When you encourage someone, it might have to deal with you yelling, yes. However, in the same sense, it's positive energy transferred from one body to another. Merely yelling negative energy to another person isn't productive unless you desire to make that person react negatively or eventually depart from the situation...you. Ex: "Baby, I know you can do it. Look at all the amazing things you've done in the past! My baby is awesome! You know what, if and WHEN you finish this, I'll not only be there to give you a full body massage but I'm personally going to cook your favorite meal then buy you something that will make you smile. Do it, baby! I know YOU can. I wouldn't love you so much if I didn't think this one task could defeat MY man! Let me know what YOU need to get it done and I'll do what I can to make it happen because I love you and want to

35

see YOU succeed! My handsome man! " That's encouragement. Inside, it was yelling positive energy and if you look deeper, the speaker also gave opportunity for help.

Help is a vital part of leadership. If your teacher only said, "You can do it. If you need further instruction...you're on your own" in some cases, it may work if the teacher is teaching a particular lesson in independence. However, if your goal is to inspire, then you may want to be there to help the person get to their finish line. You don't have to help, but offering it gives hope that, "If I fall, I have a parachute."

Now, an example of aggravation would go as follows, "YOU BETTER DO IT! After how long we've been together, I've seen you do more for stupid things. You are getting on my nerves being so lazy! I'm sick of it! Ugh! Just get it done! I'm not a babysitter! I'm not here to keep saying the SAME THINGS over and over again! You are making me not want to be here and I'm almost done with you! Man, you get on my last nerves! Neve should've dated a sorry man like you!" Now, without much analysis, you can detail the man who's receiving this message isn't ingesting positive energy. To add, just imagine if this same type of message, including energy, was thrown at the receiver on a daily or weekly basis. Would they enjoy being in such an environment? This is an aggravation to men. Being told what to do and in such a condescending manner or tone is destructive and not constructive. Men are very sensitive creatures.

We may appear to be the strong and powerful sex but in reality, we cry, hurt and wound too. Our aim is to love you and love you we shall but injuring us with words will leave scars, which create reasons to leave the "scarer".

When you're encouraging change, be the favorite teacher you've always loved. Be the instructor who rewards successful attempts, moves into the right direction and one who makes change a fun need. Help make this a challenging journey that will meet a happier existence.

When "Changing Him" remember he must also believe the change is necessary and coupled with great encouragement. He'll enjoy rising to the need. Many people need to workout for the sake of...living. *About 300,000 people die each year from being obese or overweight, this is second only to smoking.* -Eric Schlosser on CBS HealthWatch. Amazingly, we have friends, lovers or relatives of those same people spending over *$110 billion year on fast food*- Fast Food Nation. How are these companies inspiring you to eat...death? Well...marketing. *The Golden arches are now*

36

more widely recognized than the Christian cross and Children often recognize the McDonald's logo before they recognize their own name.
-Fast Food Nation.

If you want to inspire change, make your encouragement enticing. Give incentives, make it easy to attain ONLY after spending something and make it fun.

As children, we always enjoyed McDonald's. We couldn't wait to lose our minds in the ball pit and eat something called a, "Happy" meal. You can be a McDonald's to him. It will only make you a happy owner and him...a happy former employee and now co-owner.

The key in this also lies into whom you have hired to share your establishment. If they are an "underworld" worker, you may be in a battle harder than expected.

Chapter 8:
Drug Dealers Are Hard To Change...

**It's not that a man can't be changed by a woman,
it's a matter of if you're worth it and if he wants to.
~ Egypt**

Chapter 8:
Drug Dealers Are Hard To Change...

High, horny and fertile. Young, goalless and rebellious. Money, cars and women. The fast life. These traits make her wet, attentive and excited. She will and does accept this man as a product of, "Yes I can." Without a moments thought she donates her body, time and energy to this creature. When she's done, her eggs are fertilized, she can drive his cars, become the, "Main chick", have his baby, meet his mom yet all the while never realizing...this is her pinnacle to him. Pregnant and a girlfriend to a drug dealer.

Once pregnant, she becomes not a mother...but a statistic. Another woman with a baby who may enter this world not knowing their father but knowing his name. Another woman who may see a ring across her eye instead of on her finger. Another woman condemning her child by opening up to someone who has the potential to be something but instead she settled for the potential...that never became proven.

The common excuse for drug dealing is, "There weren't any other ways to make an honest buck" or "I needed to help my family". The common end for a drug dealer is either death of physical, soul or spirit from selling poison to your people and incarceration, which puts you in a position to never work a truly honest job. Thus spinning our young men in a web of low budget warehouse, stocking or other laborious positions. Which for someone who hadn't worked before, can break under the pressure of authority, low pay for hard work and lack of enjoyment. If you add the financial deductions from child support and their possible casual drug habit... he is stuck and so is she.

They never will become more than dating, no matter what she believes, she will just be a single mother. Some rare cases are too rare to even mention. Such brings sad and unrealistic hopes to women. The "game" won't inspire him to exchange more than just sex, money and fun. He can't give her anymore because the lifestyle doesn't believe in marriage, honor and love.

The love offered in this life prevents true love. He can't provide protection of her soul, heart and spirit. Who cares that he has a gun and street credit or is the biggest dealer on the block? She will need something his mindset can't comprehend. Love.

Love that will be there in the morning to hug, kiss and console her. He can't afford too much of such because being "sensitive" is only a facade he minimally exudes privately then hides publicly to prevent him exposing his softness. At least the money will be there when he isn't.

She can only live hood/drug rich for so long then a lifetime as a single mother doomed to pass on such a motto to her children. Regulated to be a "Ride or Die Chick" to a man who will eventually not be able to afford a car, has no direction and while behind bars be closer to a figment of her child's imagination than a living figure.

There are new drug dealers born on the streets daily. From meth, weed to heroine, our boys are being prepared to involuntarily abandon their children or girlfriends. It's an easy job, without many requirements but many quick benefits.

The boys will think it's cool to sell drugs before even exploring the idea of college. Despite so many stories of people coming out of the hood and becoming something, they will deny those truths for lies like, "drugs are my only way out". Sadly, they stay in. Never reaching the gifts they were born with, just accepting the demons they're surrounded by. Destined to be in jail alongside his father, another deadbeat dad or dead from a drug deal gone bad. The rewards seem to outweigh the risk.

Beautiful women, attention and fast money are the gifts of this life. Why go to college for four years only to be in debt for 10? Why spend time being a broke college student when you can have more money than a professor? Why work hard for your money when you can grind easy and out-do the college boy? What about these amazing women you get without even having a future?

Many girls are hyped at the hood life. The low pants, tattoos, roughness, pretty cars and carelessness for authority will arouse her. It doesn't matter if she's a genius she'll stupefy herself to think, "Yes I can" in the terms of changing or dealing with him. In the end, she'll just be another single mother with a child whose father is a dope peddler. The only thing to stop this is prayer, guidance and for parents to really wake up. They have to understand that encouraging words for actions towards this behavior is fruit for an impressionable young child to think, "If my other thinks it's okay...it is." Remember, parents are their first role models. Sadly, if they fail, they fail them.

Parents must let their little girls know, "Changing a drug dealer is a task that God should do, not you." This is why the first part of FEP-C ® is Faith". You must use God in this battle. Why? If you could make 4,000$ a week, what would make you stop to make 400$ every two weeks? The EP-C® formula can work for drug dealers as well. However, if they are too deep in the drug game, don't place you over the money and can't fathom a life without fast cash, you will run the risk of changing yourself before you change him. Much like the poem in the beginning of this book. If you aren't more important than the money, you will take second place or no place.

A drug dealer is sometimes like another form of bad boy. Trapped in a world where doing what's wrong is right only until you realize it was wrong. The realization of wrong is usually at the cost of your youth, freedom and leaving a child to repeat a cycle of fatherless existence. If you want to change them, know that this isn't an easy task but it's definitely possible.

If you want to change them, prepare your mind for a journey unlike a woman who is asking a man to open doors regularly. If you want to change him, pray. Pray for him, pray for yourself and pray that God will instill faith in you to stand up against logic to bring this brother back to Him. If anyone can get drug dealers off the streets, it's women. Get him off the street and into church, mosque or temple. You can be the difference between his life, death and salvation.

43

Chapter 9:
Bad boys and Good men:
In the war for a good woman's heart...
who's really friend or foe?

Change occurs at the core of, "desire". Ask him if he desires to change first. That starts it all.
~ Egypt

Bad boys and Good men:
In the war for a good woman's heart ...who's really friend or foe?

"Bad boys aint no good...good boys aint no fun" -Mary J Blige. In this civilized society much of our thinking is quite primitive. We've come a long way but have displayed an inability to refrain from glorifying poison. Give a child celery and they refuse. Bribe the child with a candy bar and they'll devour the celery. This is a day when good is belittled and bad is given positively poetic prizes. Ex: Being a smart and obedient student gains you ridicule but failing while confidently rebelling against your teacher gives you an enormous amount of popularity.

The bad boy is winning hearts, minds and bodies all across America. Leaving in his wake a multitude of regretful, broken and depressed women; many of whom are now single mothers. This is the aftermath of his irresponsible nature, excuse-ridden mouth and foul sense of manhood. As it goes, good men finish last but in this race, the good man is aiming to be the last in her heart...not the first. Let's explore the battle between bad boys and good men then you will see why changing them both can be the key in saving a woman's heart.

Before we engage in this topic, let's explore what is a bad boy or good man. Typically many are confused in this description. Bad boys are generally detailed to be irresponsible and rebellious men whom haven't or don't care to reach their full potential. Good men are almost the exact opposite. In them, you will find a desire to be responsible, respect for authority by their attention to rules and an ambitious inner gall to meet their full potential. One can make you feel like a woman and the other will make you feel like a woman who is now an adopted mother of an adult male.

Our sick sad society has cleverly conspired to keep women in funky tandem with dating men who don't deserve them and tenaciously avoiding men who do. Bad boys need women who will tend to their needs. This is a play on a woman's "nurturing" trait. The sheer innate ability to help, care for and heal works against them. If a man doesn't have to be a man to gain your love, he will never grow up...because he doesn't have to. The bad boy isn't growing up any time soon because he knows if he does, he runs the risk of losing good women. So when boys skip class, sell drugs or engage in promiscuity, they do so with an awkwardly phenomenal understanding, "I'm still going to get a good woman, no matter how bad I live". For the wrong woman, a good man isn't any better.

Although a good man appears to be what a woman needs, should want or has dreamed of, in this day, it's far too inconsistent with media teachings. Women have been taught a basic understanding, "Good men are too serious". In essence, bad boys are vacations and good men are careers. With this mindset, it makes good men seem more of an irksome hassle than a blessing. It is here where good men lose early in the battle for a woman's heart. If you are seen as someone who doesn't find excitement in acting childish, you're perceived as being "too serious". Ex: Rather than hitting a pub or bar on a study night the day before an exam he stays in. If he does go out, when everyone is having drinks, he takes water. Aiming to avoid decay in his image by being drunk around potential employers or getting into a fight courtesy of his post-alcohol induced belligerent nature. What happens is his apparent lack of attention to the moment impedes his appeal to some women. Good men care more about their futures than their present. Most successful men plan their lives by 5-10 year steps. Bad boys are reluctant to plan a 3-hour agenda let alone a 5-10 year life calendar. It's not in their makeup to act on the moment each time, but to strategize their lives effectively to create a life where they can live without worry of finances, housing or security. The "boring" title is always associated with "responsible". It's not that good men don't have fun, it's that their fun won't always cause regret.

Each culture has a reason as to why they indulge in bad boys and good men. Most of this is traditional or age inspired. Traditionally speaking, it's common for young girls to date men who aren't best for them. It's almost acceptable. Yet, also common, you'll find the woman getting pregnant by this male and adding the burden of children upon their lives; further complicating their future. As age sets in, women tend to realize the importance of good men and grow distaste for bad boys. When it comes to the future, children and finances, there is nothing grander than a good man. If the woman hasn't matured to fully extinguish wishful wanting of bad boys, she'll also take part in an age-old tradition. Domestic abuse.

White, Hispanic/Latino and Black women are all competing in a battle to survive the silent holocaust of domestic violence. Bad boys are the normal offenders of this heinous crime. When a boy doesn't grow to understand how to handle his conflicts, disagreements or rejection, he tends to use anger as communication. This trade off is tamable but largely

48

nwise to attempt, as any woman who dates a violent man runs the risk of being a victim of maiming or murder.

Good men aren't excused from this act but aren't known for gambling their livelihood over an argument. They will rather agree to disagree, resist the discussion or resolve the matter without physical harm. Women, in general, date bad boys for reasons most men don't understand. In my belief, they are actually doing it to look for leaders.

When you break a bad boy down, you actually get a demented form of a leader. A leader is someone who rebels against the norm, is respectful of authority but not commanded by it and able to take personal responsibility in directing their lives by avoiding excuses. Think about Jesus, Rev. Dr. Martin Luther King Jr. or Malcolm X. All of these men match the above description. Only the bad boy has one attractive quality, which puts him on another plateau...he doesn't care about his potential to lead.

By not being interested in doing what she knows he can do, it's an intriguing site to see. Imagine Michael Jordan only laying up the ball yet effortlessly winning games. Won't you keep watching hoping he'll dunk it? Same idea. By them not being concerned about being the man she knows he can be, it's almost entertaining riding the roller coaster of doubt as he keeps getting closer to doing something more than the bare minimum. This is even seen in the classroom.

I've watched as teachers almost shed tears when the "at risk" youth finally answered a question correctly. The young man who makes all A's, does his work and is polite won't be remembered. He's supposed to succeed and thus makes his actions not worthy of a raised eyebrow but the troubled youth may receive an extra point for just trying. We never ask if either of the boys live in the same neighborhood or have the same number of adult figures in home. I'm proof.

3.66 G.P.A in college, 7 different club executive boards, started my own college club (most active club to date), Dean's List and Phi Theta Kappa Honors yet...I received a balloon and cake at my graduation. Meanwhile my cousin, who got out of prison for a crime he was guilty of, received a block party. I lived in the hood, actually right behind a funeral home on a crack infested street and polluted lake. This was adjacent to his home. He had a father and mother in his life. I didn't have a dual parent home yet people thought I grew up with a silver spoon in my mouth. No one asked, they just assumed. Isn't it sadistic that we assume people who choose to do the right things don't deserve praise? This is the struggle.

Many good boys end up bad boys because they realize there isn't any attention for being good. We are driven by attention, praise and prize. Why do anything if no one notices? Most young boys don't think about integrity. It's about positive reinforcement. If being good isn't valued, then it's an endless road...heading nowhere. Women are the number one encouragers in this cycle.

From the clothes we wear to the attitude we portray, men are scratching and searching for ways to please their female counterparts. If being a bad boy is what they want, then that's what they become.

Remember when skinny jeans were only for women? This growing resurgence of skintight wear isn't brought upon by men but the women who date men who dress in this fashion. Whatever women like, whomever they date and wherever they frequent, we want to learn, become or reside. It's simple. If you see a woman who is dating a fool, you probably wouldn't approach her using a PhD vocabulary. You would do or say what will work. This is how men think. We don't read books on how to gain female attention, we just watch. If having tattoos on our neck, living with our parents and never truly committing to being an adult is what my friend does but he's always dating highly educated, attractive and well to do women...why would I spend 4-11 years in college? It doesn't make sense.

In all cultures, more men graduate high school than college. Many don't have a need for college, advanced learning or trade. You can work a 9-5, barely make ends meet, squander your responsibilities yet still gain the heart, mind and vagina of a great woman. It's sad, scary and true.

My friend whom I'll call, "Joker" and I had a great conversation while we drove from one of my presentations. This friend just got out of jail, has no license or permanent living arrangements yet...has a multitude of women. Add to the fact he has no college education, job or car but is the father of two children from two different women. One of the women makes over $100,000 a year. These aren't lowly, street or dumb women. These are brilliant mothers; good women with amazing hearts who made a decision to open their legs to a man with nothing.

I've asked him, "Don't they know you have nothing?" He laughed and states, "Yeah. All I have is a good stroke." What makes it more interesting is he is good at making women laugh and since he doesn't ave a job, he can donate time to their beckon call. Thus, when you put the story together, it goes as such: If you have a good stroke, free time and jokes, you can get a good woman with 6-figures. This may not be true to you, but to many good men, that's all we see.

My best friend is a marine, pilot and owns a degree from the great Bethune Cookman University. This young brother has no children, is deemed attractive by many women and stands at about 6 feet. Not only is this a God fearing brother, this is a single brother who matches most of the "Man of my dream" lists women give me during sessions. What makes him important to this story? He can't get a good woman if she fell out of the sky, into his arms and in a ready-made wedding dress.

In contrast, the "Joker" can't beat the women off of him. The "Joker" hasn't committed to any mother of his children, nor does he plan to. You know why? He doesn't have to. It's his prerogative, blessing and option. I've seen this scenario play out time and time again. A woman with everything dates a man with nothing and is left with nothing.

When you place the two on a nationwide survey of who is marriage material, overwhelmingly the Marine should win. In reality, society has curtailed many minds to give the underachiever a chance. "Why give him a chance at your heart?" is the common thinking amongst good men. Why give someone who doesn't deserve you a chance to prove they don't deserve you? This is a question I ask many women but the answers are found in their youth, upbringing or traditional excuses such as, "Good men don't approach me" or "I can't find a good man". Neither is a reason to date garbage. "Good things come to those who wait" is not just a nice phrase but reality.

A baby takes 9 months. If the gestation period is 5 or 6 months, the child could become deformed, premature or stillborn. There is no rush to love or date but as long as such a common mindset exists, then the bad boy will win.

You see, the bad boy isn't in a rush to grow up because if he does, he will run the risk of losing the edge of childlike behavior, noncommittal stress free dating and female attention. Good men take longer to grow. While he may have a greater sense of obligation towards his responsibilities, he is not without flaw.

When you're not ready to play husband, you don't fake it. During halftime between the teams, Youthful Antics and Husband Material, there are times when he will experiment with many things he may regret later in

51

life. He is guilty of making mistakes in drugs, dating multiple women, and academic production...etc. The good man has to become the man who is an outstanding man through trials, tribulations and teaching. Yet, he still good just exhibiting qualities that don't best resemble who he will become.

In this period, he may entertain women but never fully commit until he's prepared for marriage or exclusivity. Additionally, the woman he chooses must be prime material for wifehood.

While many are passionate about being worthy of a good man, their actions don't reflect qualities good men attend to. Good men would have sex with bad girls but seldom marry one. As you venture towards the "Conviction" chapter you'll note, it's important for you to be what you are and never fake it.

Good men pay attention to what you say, do and don't do. They are keen to such because "deal breakers" are golden ways to preserve this definitive decision on a female counterpart. If you want a good man but date bad men or can't give up actions you know aren't that of a wife, a good man won't approach you. They fear wasting time with a girl claiming to be a woman. Much like some good women with their head on straight won't entertain young men who act foolish.

I've had women who post semi-nude pictures online, use profanity in social media boards and aren't clearly prepared for life after college yet can't figure out why the men who are drawn to them...only want sex. It's simple; good men make life investments in women. Bad men only gamble their days for sex with a woman.

If you were investing your life into someone, wouldn't you be a little slow to place all your chips in them? You would probably analyze your cards to ensure it won't be time wasted. Good men seemingly are a treat for patient women who not only know their worth but also won't lower it. Bad men are for anyone who loses faith in their prayers for a good man.

White, Hispanic and Black women are guilty of lowering their standards for bad boys. However, each culture didn't originally own a true voice or choice in standards. Historically speaking, women have only really been "valid" Americans for about 60-70 years. In this period (Before Mid 1900's) they were true second-class citizens and as you'll read later in further detail, not even allowed to vote. Thus, if he had a home, land and an ability to feed her, he was the husband. That didn't make him a good man because he could provide. Honestly, many were not. Between the ack of respect for a woman's voice, inability to gain equal wage or children out of wedlock, you saw much abuse in these homes.

Domestic abuse is still a horrible epidemic in this land; now imagine the more primitive America. Essentially, women had no choice to date a man of character over a man who could provide. Hopefully he had both but if not, why choose the one where you will starve? From here, you can note media images of rebels and the tough workingman became the model husband. Nothing was intuitively mentioned about his faith, integrity or ability to love a woman. You were only given an example of "Real men work, don't cry or complain." Such a description didn't allow for sensitivity of inner concerns or the concerns of your love interests.

Many women were married back then but how many were in happy marriages? How many stayed because divorce for "bad treatment" was looked down upon and not found in the Holy Bible? How many stayed because if they left there would be no one to feed their children since women didn't provide for households until relatively recent? This is how many American women began to date and find uncomfortable contentment with men who nowadays would live in a jail for abuse.

They lived in a time when this silent crime was only heard by their children, friends and family. Rarely did anyone tune into the evil acts committed upon these women. Bad boys won that battle but as we grew as a society, so did our definitions of love and expression.

While all women were traditionally pushed to accept what was available, Black women have the same argument but an additional historical reasoning for humoring bad boys.

Black Women's love affair with Bad Boys

She was forced to watch her husband being tied to two horses, both heading in separate directions. Then the animals were ferociously beaten until they ripped the man in half. She was forced to see her husband brutally flogged* if he ever stood up against the masters' will, desires or to defend his wife. She was forced to see her husband shipped to another plantation if he seemed too strong or had the makeup of a "Salt Water African"*. Those Africans who refused to succumb to being slaves.

These Africans embodied...leadership qualities slave owners feared. They were typical, "good men" who wanted to defend, support and raise children with this Black Woman. Such scared the slave owners and thus inspired their actions.

Against her will, she had no choice but to see, live and hate this. Willie Lynch* devised a way to break the Black family by making the man invisible and the woman the head. If he was always sold, made to mate with another woman or traded, how could he be a father, lover and provider? This woman was an adapter. Her only reaction was to pay more attention to her son and protect him as much as she could to prevent the same scenario from occurring. It was then when the Black woman feared loving the strong Black man and began her love affair with boys.

Do you wonder why current hip-hop artists are loved by women? Why would a grown woman who has goals, security and a future even wear a shirt stating, "Free (Insert guilty Black rapper's name)"? Why would she support him with her attention, money or even date someone who resembles him? Can you truly regulate your thought to, "She likes bad boys"? If so, then you're right. Bad boys.

Notice how many rappers dress like kids? Many rarely wear suits unless they're at an awards show (sometimes), funeral or in the courtroom They dress in such attire because the Black man is absent. A man teaches his son 1 Corinthian 13:11* "...When I became a man, I put childish ways behind me"

His son realizes that once he's no longer a child...he has to dress and behave like a man. However, either by choice, circumstance or reluctance many young boys never become men.

They not only dress like boys, they behave like them. When a child wants a new toy, they badger their mother for such a toy but when the toy is no longer fun, they abandon it. Now, parlay that into the behavior of a young man today. He will sweet talk and even date a young lady. Sex is the fun portion of this journey. Yet, when a baby arrives, he will abandon his obligation. He won't endure the trials of rearing a child because it's a responsibility and is no longer fun. Now reflect on the many men who give up on their children. These aren't men, but boys. The problem presented too many factors or hardship and rather than enduring their responsibility, they refused to accept it then gave it away to the world. Sadly, these men are deemed, "desirable" by many of our sisters, not all.

The Black woman is a boy's first nurse. The one who quieted his tears with attention, love and comfort. This was her employment in his life. As long as she cared for him, he would stay and love her. The modern day

...ad boy is exactly an older version of a baby boy. They have little responsibilities beyond making babies, sex and eating. Many live with their parents until 35+, have no permanent legal career or are able to consistently maintain a relationship. Minus 10 or 20 from his age and you can't imagine this being a grown man but he is such.

Bad boys give the Black woman an inferiorly insidious form of comfort. As the good Black man was disregarded as someone who would eventually leave her, she knew as long as she nurtured the bad boy, he would stay. Oddly, she was right. He would stay. He would stay in many disgusting forms. From a deadbeat father, prison inmate #2345 or the man who "used and abused me". You rarely hear grand stories of this young stallion who was nothing and became something courtesy of his female only to grow with, marry and bring children to her. No. You probably have never heard such a fable.

Black bad boys are the poison Black women willingly infect themselves with. The lethal poison which slowly decays her spirits, hopes and dreams only to make real how destructive her decision-making was to her heart. Black men are damaged in this ordeal solely because they aren't allowed to be what a Black woman needs and if they are, they are scrutinized, analyzed and denied at their first mistake.

The good Black man has been mocked over the years and made to live in contradiction. In order to avoid human error, they tiptoe through life while still losing their prize. They can't be too tough, sexual or decisive or they run the risk of running a good woman away. If they are too cool, they are deemed, "players" and undesirable. If they poise too much of a threat to her independence, the woman will ignore him as, "not my type".

He's regulated in a position of, "Guy friend" or "Just my friend" and forced to listen to her whine about how this evident bad boy destroyed her self-esteem, trust and heart. All the while, as he hears these stories of how she wants a God fearing, good and honest man, he's stuck making passive jokes, "Well, I'm all those things...wish you would consider me (he jokingly coughs)." She won't acknowledge him until he is taken, she's no longer attractive or when she awakens courtesy of another painful relationship with someone she shouldn't have allowed in her life.

The Black, Hispanic or White women who refuse dating deadbeat men are titled, "Uppity, Too Good or Too Picky". Deadbeat men are typically those who care not about their outward appearance, future or social responsibilities and may not be the ideal mate to bear a child with. Now, amazingly these will be the women who either bend around the age 27-30 to dating a bad boy, become lesbian only to harm a true lesbian with the infamous "I thought I was gay" speech or who will hold out, stay in shape and enjoy life only to be married to someone who meets her standards. The good man who awaits her will be ready, prepared and eager to satisfy her, as a woman should be satisfied. This is all courtesy of his durability.

Good men grow a thicker than steel coat of skin which bad boys aren't able to fathom owning. Many bad boys are aware of this skin, which is why many bad boys respect businessmen. They can see it takes more to live with the skin of integrity, purpose and ambition than the opposite. Bad boys are liberal in their lifestyles by comparison. It's because they will never become true victims of what Good men are victims of.

A good man lives on the sharpest double-edged sword. He can't succumb to most human instincts, no matter if those actions are what everyone would exercise.

Ex: Imagine if a much shorter and smaller stranger walks up to someone you love and says to them, "I hate you and your people!" then punches, spits on and begins to demean them with derogatory words. After this initial assault, they commence with beating them maniacally. As your loved one is lying on the ground covered in their own blood, what will you do?

A. Jump in between them and defend your loved one with harsh words.
B. Jump in between them and defend your loved one with your fists.
C. Jump on your loved one, absorb the assailant's blows and wait patiently for the police.

Keep in mind; this is someone you love who is inches away from being erased from this earth. You have 3 choices, which do you choose? Amazingly, when doing this scenario, most chose B. Utilizing the reasoning, "If I don't stop them, they will kill them. Words won't do anything to a crazy person. If I took the blows, I could die as well."

You know what? You would be correct if you chose B...if you were anyone but a Good man.

Take that same scenario and insert the word "President" instead of you. The entire story changes. Imagine if the President jumped on the First Lady and cussed out an assailant? What if you saw the President of the Free World beating someone much smaller to a bloody pulp or losing in a fight to someone much smaller? The media would take their actions and deem the President, "Violent, primitive or a thug". Now, if the President died defending the First Lady with his life...he's a hero.

Good men live in a conflicting world. They can't act on their natural impulses but are deemed "soft" if they don't act aggressive and "crazy" if they do. This is where they become victims. Many women want good men to be the opposite of what a good man is. "Honest, kind but...with an edge." It's comparable to buying a Lamborghini and wanting it to have features of a 94' Civic. It's confusing.

Add insult to injury, the media will incite women to believe good is bad and bad is good thus further highlighting how confused our society is. Don't believe me? Have you noticed good men are deemed "boring, too busy or weak" but bad men are praised for being "fun, protective and sexy"? If so, then the media has done grand job of making that connection.

Bad boys aren't as dumb as many play them to be. These males have figured women out. They are wise enough to know how to toy with women.

Bad boys don't intimidate good women. That's why some women love them. Thus, bad boys play the "challenge" card. They will always unconsciously fail at something, refuse to meet their full potential or resist treating a woman the way THEY know she deserves to be treated. You see, it is here where these males know a woman's desire to upgrade, change and defeat equations will work against her.

The bad boy will splash in a waste hole of excuses only to scuba dive into stories of what they could be if they only had a chance. No matter the age or situation, they will play her like a fiddle for years. Friends, family and outsiders can inspire her to realize, "He isn't changing at all" but she won't listen. She'll endure his antics without any resolve but hope he will "get it together soon". Which he will not. Remember, he doesn't have to.

Who would pay for gas when they have an unlimited gas pump at home? I wouldn't. When she attempts to enforce a call to action, the bad boy will simply toss another reason as to why her request is too much: Either vomiting stories of his upbringing, how hard it is or something he'll do when ready.

Excuses are what boys use to continue doing what they know shouldn't be done. Plain and simple. Many of the men I've counseled aren't 18 but 25-35. When should women ignore the age-old excuses of, "I didn't have a father, I was raised like this or I don't know any other way to behave"? Answer: Not any time soon. As long as becoming a man is an option, why take it? Real men man up because they should, not because they are told to.

I lost my mother at 12 and was abandoned by my father. My first 3 years of college, I entered as an actual registered orphan. Almost every year of my life I've been in one neighborhood to the next. Where's my excuse? I lived in the hood. I got arrested, sold drugs and fought on the streets. You know the difference? I stopped when I turned 17. It wasn't some magical awakening but a realization of, "That's wrong and I can't have a future acting as such."

For each early release or exam day in high school, I would wear a funky outfit. They were always goofy, wild and unpredictable. My last day of high school I wore a dress shirt, tie, slacks, belt and held a briefcase. People asked, "What are you trying to be, a businessman?" I replied, "No, a college student". This was the mindset of a 17 year old who was no better off than any hustler who can cry about his upbringing.

I had to see my mother placed in a casket before I fully reached puberty. None of my family stuck together. Instead of attempting to take me in, they wanted to put my younger sister and me in foster care. This was my life. I was supposed to be the "bad boy" but I made a decision. I refused to be the same man who hurt my sister. These boys saw their mothers disheveled by the actions of their fathers but yet; they repeated them to another young lady. This is a choice. They chose to be deadbeat fathers. How can you blame your absent father for you being a horrible dad? He's absent. You can't blame someone who isn't there for what you do. It's simple. I can't blame the police for my speeding ticket. I sped. It's a choice. Men choose ways to better their futures. Good men are created, not born.

Good men are constructed out of necessity and choice. Young men who were tired of watching their mothers cry, who wanted to be proud men like their fathers or were disgusted at the idea of being like their fathers. When I wrote this, my intent was to inspire bold women of all hues to understand how powerful they are. This choice in changing a bad boy into a decent man or tweaking a good man into a better man is all in what you decide. Just remember you have the choice. We don't live in the 1920's any longer. You have a part in your pain and happiness.

Any man can be changed...any man can be made better. Some aren't worth the energy, some are. In the end, it's your choice to make. You can't force yourself to date outside of your type but you can force yourself to love yourself enough to know...you deserve the best piece of clay to mold into a great work of art. Your energy, your life...your choice.

*Flogged:
Whipped

*Salt Water Africans:
Africans who were fresh from Africa. Known for being unruly, unbreakable and able to incite others to follow their lead.

*Willie Lynch:
Deviser of the Willie Lynch letter, which taught how to break slaves, teach slaves to trust White people and distrust Blacks in addition to hating one another but loving the Whites.

*1 Corinthian 13:11
"When I was a child, I talked like a child, I thought like a child, I reasoned like a child. When I became a man, I put childish ways behind me"

Chapter 10:
Why Independent Women Have Changed Men...
But Can't Change Men

"EGYPT"

There is a man who can love you right. However, if you allow Mr. Wrong to occupy your time, you will never meet him. ~ Egypt

Chapter 10:
Why Independent Women Have Changed Men... But Can't Change Men.

Starving, near dead and desperate, the giraffe stares at an apple atop one tree. Rather than dying, this animal stretches its neck as high as it can, reaches the apple and defies death. Others in the same state watch this only to realize, "in order to survive...we have to adapt".

As the harsh seasons progressed and food became even scarcer, the giraffes with longer necks lived and those who refused to endure the pain of stressing their bodies...died off. It's evolution.

We see today on Animal Planet and zoos across the world, these long necked healthy living creatures that survived, adapted and are now able to extend their family trees. How does this relate to why Independent women have changed men...but can't change men?

A man will become what he needs to become so he can cum... period. Through evolution, we realized that if we had food and shelter, we could entice women to live with us. Thus, we worked and built to fit a woman's basic needs. In today's world, who are the construction workers, architects and employers? Yes, women are involved in these industries but men heavily outnumber them. We became whatever women deemed, "desirable" even if women don't really desire it. Sometimes we say what we want but actions speak louder than words.

We have always done what was necessary for our survival. If we had to be swift and wise enough to outwit predators or prey, we would. As long as it would bring you safety, food and...us. It was part of our makeup to gain a woman. We have no limits on what we would do for women. This evidence dates back to the dawn of time. The Holy Bible is riddled with stories of how men disobeyed God to please their thirst for women.

David sent a woman's husband to the front of the battle lines to die so David could have his wife. Solomon began to adore alternate gods courtesy of his attention to other women. Adam bit an apple and directly disobeyed God. All of these are exact ancient examples of how powerful

63

our desire to appease women goes.

We only have two goals in life: Reaching a higher power and obtaining a woman...period. Everything you can add to the everyday life of man is attached to one of those goals. We don't buy cars, get jobs or workout to solely please ourselves. Dig deeper. We are motivated by those two objectives.

As years progressed, you would note many women would be married, with homes and full families, including the stereotypical Golden Retriever. For decades we have been winning in the terms of women having a man at home who is a worker aiming to keep the family together and a woman who is able to live without worry. However...many factors have changed. Both parties share blame and also the answers.

Around the 1980's- mid 1990's a great "independent woman" movement entered our minds but shortly became mutated into a destructive form by a delusional, misadjusted and poorly led society. This was a very illustrious and grand idea for a woman who wasn't considered "important" until...spots during/after World War 1 and definitely after World War 2 when men were dying.

It was after World War II when they were left to be mothers, servants and not able to do anything but work. It was then where women had a chance to own a voice in America. It was then when they began to prove the age old, "Whatever a man can do, I can too." However, men wanted women to believe they were weak and nothing. This propaganda-induced brainwashing was inspired by fear. Elite men feared women would understand their comparability to men. Which then would inspire fear amongst men. Imagine, they outnumber men, can multitask better than most of them and live longer. Such would be an over formidable foe. However, like the slave, the woman was treated like a second-class citizen. Pay them less, work them more.

Women watched as they did the same job as a man, took care of a household and maintained their livelihood without a male present. This is what fed the true "Independent woman". During Woman's Suffrage Movement women banned together and silently screamed with their actions, "I'm your sister, mother, lover, aunt and grandmother, not your footstool. I deserve equal right to vote". Remember, this is the same woman who received her right to vote after Black male slaves. The same Black male who was only worth 3/5ths of a White male. This woman stood up and demanded what any human in America should receive.

After years of turmoil, they are almost there. Hilary Clinton was a whisper away from being the first female president. Her ascent was courtesy of the untainted version of the independent campaign.

She was leading because she was the worthy candidate despite her gender. The "I can because I am woman" can't be missed in her makeup. Hilary was the epitome of strength. As she stood, many women who were forced to sit, sat taller so Hilary could gain height amongst their beaten shoulders. The movement was in Mrs. Clinton. This is what it's supposed to inspire. Millions of future presidents. Hilary Clinton is a direct beneficiary of the women who started the independent woman's movement. Yet, what was aimed to be a needed movement became infected with media induced misdirection to turn the purity of this idea into a passing fad and the resulting consequence of what it is...today.

Rather than inspiring women to understand, "You have all the tools a man has. There is no need for you to submit yourself as inferior to another human being. What he can do, you can do. In the end, you two are equal. Lastly, you two need each other to provide areas of learning for your children and selves that one can't/shouldn't do alone" the common motivation was, "You can do bad all by yourself. You don't need a man. Get yours before they do." Having this kind of a mindset has ruined something that was proposed to be encouraging to our community.

From the early to mid 90's the heavy untainted Independent woman movement was what many needed to supplement the successful Woman's Suffrage campaign. The media has a way of making you think what you shouldn't and utterly fogging a clear message.

Women have grown from that decade to have better jobs, higher pay and greater levels of self-esteem in comparison to the early 1900's. Many are enjoying life without a man as a superior. Now their main opponent to the challenges in life is not really men but themselves.

Men aren't as formidable as previously...because they aren't in battle with women. The war is now fought on a different plateau. Some women aren't paying sight to what society is doing. Their battle has manifested into a waste of time...since they're at war with an invisible mirror. While many think they must defeat the man and show him "I can too" they in turn give an open door towards a painful long-term problem.

While aiming to prove herself, many a time, she would defeat her male nemesis and acquire positions never owned by females. Allowing your higher levels of estrogen to exist in places a woman was probably never allowed. Yet...when she aged and tried to date...something eerily destructive occurred. Door opens...welcome Long Term Pain Sr.

When some of those women entered the latter stages of their childbearing age, their biological clocks would tick past, "I'm almost too old to have a baby". Then rather than focusing on obtaining the best co-parent, it was more important to live on the "I want a baby" hill. While many of them have been anti-BS, not taking any weak or inferior man* as a mate, she found herself lonely, depressed and in an isolated corner of success without company. Regardless of the many men who accompany her ascension, be it their ethnicity, height or class, she would still feel "alone" or "too successful" to entertain the men in her direct arena. Thus the eyes began to wander toward men who only dreamt of the ladder of success. It is truly amazing how someone who is on the top of a ladder believes they have to entertain those who never climbed. One would think a man either next to, a little below or above would be fit to date but there is always an excuse or reason as to why it doesn't work.

Some women were patient enough to wait until someone on their level came. Others became tired of the waiting game and after dismal results, started to bottom feed. She realized she had enough money, power and leadership authority, she didn't need a man for such. So, a man who could provide leadership in the home, authority concerning decision making and power regarding direction...was a turn off. Not only were they "nowhere to be found" but also they weren't as thirsty, needy and available as their less successful and immature male counterparts. Additionally, being with someone who could possibly put her back in the "inferior" position would be a reverse of what she's known for years. Unwilling to do such, she resorted to "sperm donors" traditionally dubbed, "thugs, societal losers and rough necks".

Yes, the latter seems like an unfortunate choice for such a prestigious, brilliant and amazing specimen of a woman...right? However, that's completely the opposite. Those men aren't leaders and really only own directorial influence inside bed sheets. Most of those types aren't wise enough to know they don't run the woman. Yes, they may yell, scream or even physically assault them but it's just like you THINK you can drive your car because you own it. If you don't pay your car insurance or renew your tag, you can't drive the car you own. So who really has the power of your car, you or the state? This is the same idea.

Women know these men host no threat to their dominance and thus...can procreate willingly and successfully. Add to injury, these women helped inspire songs, movies, support and books for/about these men.

66

hese were dominant women urging other women to follow in their ootsteps. Ex: MC Lyte "I need a rough neck", Mary J. Blige's "Bad Boy" ong or the sheer over indulgence of love for Elvis. A clear "bad boy" type. hese men became ideal fathers and lovers. Good boys faded to the oackseat as last place finishers. Solely because they were deemed ooring, unattractive and not secure enough to donate safety...in addition o posing a major threat to female dominance.
his is how the cycle began but it's increasingly worse.

Today, some women have grown wiser. Realizing they can be equal to a man without losing their femininity, equality or identity. Many understand that allowing a man to be the head of the household doesn't make them inferior but just places them in an area where they can thrive without worry of direction, yet still have input on the journey. Sadly to some, the men they've decided to have this household or escapade with...aren't equipped to lead, inspire or support them (spiritually, socially or emotionally). These men have "got on game" to do as little as possible in the world, account for none of their potential but all the while knowing in the end...he will get a good woman. A woman with a job...no...A CAREER, goals, obtainable aspirations and security for him. All he has to offer is a rebellious attitude, excuse ridden tongue and fertile penis. The only tools needed and provided by an arousing amount of boys today.

This isn't a black thing (as evidenced by the Elvis mention) this is a national epidemic. Men have learned succeeding isn't the best way to obtain one of the two main aims we have in life. If we succeed too much, we scare off potential mates who would rather a man who needs work instead of one who can actually upgrade the women. If we care more about our futures, career and spirituality, it's a turn off because he doesn't have enough time to dedicate to a woman. Meanwhile, the loser has almost an unlimited amount of time since he isn't...doing anything. Besides the mere fact a good man is prejudged as boring, she will date a bad boy with the expectations of him being the opposite...fun, right?

Sadly, the bad boy isn't "fun" but "dramatic". With jail visits, baby momma drama, poor social skills (Ex: profanity in public), domestic violence and an inability to communicate his emotions, she considers this, "fun". Most women I've interviewed haven't been beyond bowling, movies, dinner or home movie with their bad boy beau. So, where is the "fun"? Your fun isn't true fun; it's deadly entertainment that builds nothing in you but pain, misery and self-loathing when you realize the time you've wasted with such a feeble excuse for a man.

When she attempts to alter his behavior, she runs into a double-edged sword. One such weapon that defeats almost every woman...every time. One part of the sword is the man's logic: **If I got you the way I am...why would I change to keep you?** The other part is her confused teaching. She wants him to be what she didn't fall in love with and won't love. When he attempted to make decisions, she veiled or ignored them. Now, she wants him to initiate actions and choices for the two? He's not dumb, he will figure it out. What she's teaching him is basically how to behave as a respectable human but the moment he learns how to be a man...he will leave her.

No true man is ready to be anyone's arm candy or sperm donor. At least not a respectable man who loves his woman. Boys yes but not men. Instead of leaving her, once he's grown a bit, he'll just smile and wave to get by. As he wises up, he will find a way to end this mockery of a relationship only to treat the next woman...exactly the way a woman is supposed to be treated and he will be treated like a man. Now she's back in the dating pool, (odds are with a baby) sad, bitter, angry with all men and confused as to what went wrong.

By the time she understands, "I deserve a good man" her body, face and baggage may no longer support enough attractive points for a good man. Good men enjoy beautiful and minimally drama-filled women We all have drama but a good man knows the fewer amounts she brings in, the easier his life will be. When you have went from a size 5 to 10, own permanent bags under your eyes from crying about this loser and an aggravating attitude you built from the last relationship, it is a turn off to a good man. Women amazingly believe good men are "ducks". Meaning, they don't care about looks, attitude or what you have. That's a horrible assessment of a man...period. Good or bad, beauty matters...yes. Otherwise don't you think the word wouldn't be in the Holy Bible describing people? Attitude determines your altitude. Would you date a mean, sarcastic and verbally hurtful person? Lastly, baggage is a game changer. If the person has a child they can't take care of, baby daddy who constantly enters the picture with threats yet is invited to do so and a broken woman who compares every act you do to her previous loser, that's baggage we see, take note of and run from.

Not all independent women will suffer this fate. Many will avoid this by choosing to date men who are worth their time, God-fearing leaders and not in need of wild amounts of upgrading. Men who don't use, "I never had a father" or "I was raised like this" to live the life of an abuser, womanizer or lowly man. Men who can't fathom being anything but a provider even if he shares the role with his woman. Those women who believe in and follow the above may not always land in successful

elationships, since a relationship is more than having two compatible
people. However, they will avoid leaving a relationship like many of the
above stating, "Why did I waste my time...with a waste of time?"

There is nothing wrong with being independent but understand your
role is temporary and meant to exist as temporary. God didn't create us
together for us not to live in tandem. True independence is knowing you
don't have to depend on another. Simple. However, when you engage
such an idea with the additional harsh attitude of, "I don't need
another...period" you add toxic waste to a beautiful movement.

An independent woman is one of the most gorgeous sites donated
by the Most High. She is a woman who can make you feel needed but
simultaneously without word allow you to understand...even without you,
"I'll be fine". The mention of, "without word" is most imperative. When your
actions are those of an independent person, it speaks volumes. Not
relying on gifts, money or dates to create your happiness is all part of it.
However, when someone comes in, they just add to your happy state.
They themselves aren't the sole creators of your happiness because you
were already happy before they arrived. There is no need to mention, "I
don't need you to be happy" if you were already happy prior to their
appearance. When it comes to "Changing him", if you give him notice
that his existence isn't priority because someone else can do his job or you
can yourself, he may not stay...since you just gave him no reason to stay.

This is my theory, my belief and my way of thinking. It's built over 9
years of research in counseling strangers, clients, friends, lovers and family.
If you're an independent woman, be one who isn't the "today" version.
Don't allow society or the media to infect what you are. We need you.
Without a woman, we aren't complete as men. Yes, we have the ability
to live, succeed and enjoy life but it's not at its fullness with you missing
from the equation. An independent woman of today can't change any
man in the way that will benefit her but an independent woman of
yesterday can change a man for the betterment of himself and her.

When it comes to knowing you're coming home or to visit the
woman of your dreams after a long day of hard work and she's excited to
see you as her equal, lover and co-leader, nothing compares. You will
then see why being an independent woman encourages a man to make
you happy. He will know you worked hard that day, for your own money,
own future and own happiness. He will want to relieve that stress with his
work, his faith and dedication to you. He will live a life based on pleasing
God, himself and you. If he has a woman who makes his existence
unimportant...he will change...his relationship status and date someone

who will make his voice, time and attention purposeful. It's the very of the beast. Only an independent woman of yesteryear can use FEP-C effectively.

*Inferior man:
Typically regarding his job or financial status, not his character

Chapter 11:
Are You Ready to Learn FEP-C$_®$?

Chapter 11:

Are You Ready to Learn FEP-C$_®$?

Changing a bad boy into a good man isn't the goal of every woman or this book. Showing a man how to handle a good thing…is the goal. Many women are slaves to a horrific and unsuccessful teaching which only breeds sadness and regret. Their strategy meets a sad form of success where they believe progress is made, only to realize they've lowered their standards so much that…he finally meets them. "Most people are always loyal to their patterns whether if they are conscious of them or not". -Iyanla Vanzant.

Faith, Penalty/Prize, Environmental Change and Conviction (FEP-C$_®$) are the true answers to re-scripting that pattern. These are the routes women have used for centuries to "Change Him", but until now, no one connected the dots. Also, no one ever asked a man, "How would I change you?" This book's formula is what has changed not only men but also people for centuries.

No gimmicks, no tricks, no lies. Just cold hard truths that will either leave your burning eyes riddled with unimaginable tears of joy or give the weaker female contenders a reason to fail for fun. Even the stronger women may meet momentary defeat in the journey to "Changing Him" but "Temporary defeat isn't permanent failure"-Napoleon Hill.

Thus, when the this next chapter is read and you surface belief in your amazing mind that, "I can change him", you will reshape history, your heart, hearts of others and begin to help create a world where the supply of "good" men won't matter. Since everyone will be happy being treated the way…they deserve.

The difference between being treated like a queen vs. trash is...your standard. You set it...he will follow or leave. ~ Egypt

Chapter 12:
FEP-C_®
Faith

Chapter 12:

EP-C®

Faith

It's easy to discount any reasoning regarding changing a man by simply uttering, "God changes men". Such a statement, in my opinion and experience, is undeniably true. What makes this even more powerful and relative to these provocative points inside this book is the bold question, "Are you willing to lead him and yourself to God to change him?

Who better to lead a man back to God than a woman? Women have an undeniable and seemingly insurmountable amount of influence in this area. Men are willing to follow women to the depths of hell. Church, temple or mosques are locations he will explore, if you only agree to meet him there. Have you noticed dance halls or clubs allow women in for free before a certain hour? This isn't to solely lure women but the men who have been chasing you since puberty, whose hormones now no longer permit him to label women, "yucky" but "I like her face". They spend money on drinks, clothing and shoe wear just to impress women. If a man knows a woman is only willing to meet him at church, he will attend. Once there, she has an opportunity to inspire his zest for her/their religion. This isn't a "scare" tactic, but an ideal route to laying the grounds for what she's about. He will come. Wherever she goes, he will be there because our mission is woman but if women aren't giving us the address, then how will we find her there?

Many a times, the idea of inviting a current mate or potential partner to church, temple or mosque is shot down as, "Pushy" or "A turnoff". Yet, giving your body up as reward for their attention is rarely met with those words. However, I can almost guarantee a man who is weary of attending church, temple or mosque but ready to enter your body may not love you the way you deserve to be loved. If lust were easier to express than love, why would you fear losing someone who refuses to abandon this mindset? When you invite us to come, you give God an open door to enter this man's heart, soul and mind. Faith is one trait that can only benefit the foundation of a relationship's core.

Faith gives **hope** through times of trial and uncertainty. Ever wonder why most bad relationships last longer than the good? Ex: Good relationships end over one party not making enough money or working too much. Bad relationships have an awkward assortment of horrific details, which should end the association but only stirs it. From cheating, lying, to new children from another partner, none seem to steer one from an on-again-off-again relationship. Only until it ventures into a relative catastrophic territory does it end. You see, bad relationships are riddled with an amazing amount of faith forcefully constructed from a union created in rebellion. Typically a good person will entertain someone who is his or her complete opposite or a functional walking disagreement to their standards. Despite them not being on their level, they lie to themselves as to why this person should be in their life while fully knowing they shouldn't. This begins the move in faith.

From here, they begin to go against what they believe in with **hope** it will provide a happy ending. They see the good in them and have faith there's **hope** they are just misunderstood or blame their standards for being unrealistic. As they waddle their evident and hidden flaws into her life and heart, she ignores the signs of habitual fault to give full attention to what they can be. It is here where faith commences to work out of her favor. Despite an overabundance of justification for wise departure, she has faith in the unseen. The belief that it will get better if you just stick it out. She stays, is hurt and spent nonrefundable time on someone who shouldn't have been amiss her existence. We can go on, but you see the point of faith if used in an unhealthy relationship.

Faith is the basic building block of a strong, never-ending and legendary relationship. It is with faith you can overcome income issues, depression or moments when you or your partner are struggling with any life equation. Going to church, temple or mosque is not where you find faith, but nourish it. When you institute your faith, no matter the organization, it inspires connectivity. Even atheists have faith. It may not be in a God but their car turning on, getting to work on time and the fruits of being a good person. The point is to believe in something and not shy away from involving your partner in your belief system. It is there where you two can grow in knowledge of what you believe or don't believe in. It is there where you can have a common ground to defend moments of despair with words, prayer or mediation. It is there where you can save yourself from giving up because you have someone who is as stubborn as you are and refuses to leave your side because they don't own an "I quit" faith.

How Do You Make Faith Work?

Making faith work is a dual duty. First, you must understand the job descriptions of faith. Contrary to sick traditional opinion, faith isn't "sticking it through" when you know it's not supposed to go further. We are a growingly civilized community yet we are more primitive as technology

78

eplaces common sense. No, faith isn't enduring horrible treatment, abuse or misery at the behest of God. That's a foolish route to permanent life scars. When the bad outweighs the good, you can't blame a higher power for your torment. It's a saying, "trouble don't last always" but if the next door neighbor named, Trouble is invited into your heart more so than your roommate Happiness, Trouble will lower your hearts market value. Infect yourself with these duties of faith.

. Faith is what keeps a relationship going when you aren't smiling, laughing or adoring your mate.

We don't live in a time when, "sticking together" is the popularly promoted rhetoric. (At least not for good couples.) There are times in any relationship when things aren't beautiful. They may be few and far in between but they exist. It's common and quite angelic to have solvable disagreements (that meet resolution) or times when you aren't fond of your mate. However, it is here where faith is needed.

You may inaccurately cloak this temporary ill for reason to end when such thought isn't needed or correct. Older couples mastered the art of overcoming adversity for the betterment of a relationship. You must realize all arguments aren't doors for completion. Sometimes it's an avenue to bring about never before discussed points of views, which only brighten a relationship's light of success.

2. Faith is the measuring tool used to detail if your efforts in bettering your relationship will be fruitful.

Abstaining from sex, not kissing on the first date or refuting any talk of babies without a marriage discussion prior to such conversation are examples of a faith duty. Many fear having guidelines because our mate may not meet them or be turned away due to them. However, as I speak for many of my male colleagues and myself, a woman with guidelines is more desired as a long-term mate than one who has none. Why so? If it took you nothing to obtain her attention, think of how easily someone who does something can take it away. One should not fear women with standards, it breeds integrity and value; two key components of being a choice wife and mother. In this duty, I would venture to evaluate the candidate you are in fear of losing.

No man who wants a woman who is worth something should expect her to be free. If you buy a Bentley, you should be prepared for guidelines a 1994 Honda Civic won't require. However, if you're interested in men who don't know the difference between the two cars or why he should ready himself to expend more energy on one, then this man may need time to mature.

There is nothing wrong with having standards and never dare to believe such. You owe it to yourself to have faith in what you request. Please, be honest with your guidelines. Have faith in them. Things such as not being slapped or cheated on shouldn't endure being deemed, "high class" or "stuck up" but normal...very normal. Have faith in your barometer, it only benefits you and whoever you love or will love.

3. Faith is knowing your pursuit or departure won't warrant regret.

This is the last but definitely not least important duty of faith. In many occurrences, we tend to fear the POTENTIAL bite of regret. Oddly, it's one time in our lives where we become psychic. Amazingly able to detail the future feeling or consequence we may endure courtesy of an action. Well, that is natural and very common. It's all part of being an adult.

As adults the art of accepting regret is nothing simple but a task you should believe will lessen the hardship which may follow. Regret is all part of life. The "What if" hangs over our heads since we were able to take any test. Remember any test you've taken, have you ever said, "I should've selected ___ and my score would be higher"? For many of us, the previous example is all too familiar. In this case, one should be ready for regret because, if done right, you won't regret anything at all. Whether you stay or leave, it's all about faith.

If this person isn't loving or treating you the way you deserve to be treated but you have endured what you believe is "long enough" with faith things would alter yet you ran into even harsher treatment as your hearts durability ran thin...leave. You own no badge of honor for being the person who stayed lived through betrayal, abuse and embarrassment but met no sunshine at the end of your storm. You have a choice. As stated previously, leaving when you know there was no rainbow after the flood shouldn't bring about regret but happiness. It will be hard.

Any time we loan our heart, body or spirit with another, giving up the energy is seemingly impossible. As we age, it becomes harder due to the societal influence of, "I'm too old to start over" which is a deadly lie. Women 70+ have begun new loving relationships. It's just an ugly lie to keep you miserable. In reflection to departure, understand your life is yours and yours alone. Stress can end that life. Stress is stronger than any drug or cancer available. Why? Because it's the body's poison. It ruins you from the inside. So, now imagine being with this person only to spend more time n the hospital than with them courtesy of the toxicity of their actions. Leaving can be the difference between your life and death. Have faith in what you're doing.

Just because your friends or parents are in love with the person doesn't mean you must endure all the hidden or unspoken evils that exist in the relationship. I've seen women with "Mr. Right" (In public) but in private, she's raped, beat up, cheated on, lied to and infected with diseases other women have given him. Her admittance of his actions might bring about embarrassment so she hides behind sunglasses and stories of falling down stairs. If she left, she may lose money, this perverted form of love and a warm body but at least her dignity, health and mind wouldn't stay at risk for unbearable pain. Then, your regret would be staying too long. Having faith you won't regret staying isn't as difficult as leaving but will bring about the same level of happiness.

To decipher whether staying is the ideal move rests in a simple formula of pros and cons. Can you say you're happier more than you are sad? That's it. Such an equation isn't in need of a large sermon but a simple yet direct, "Do you smile more so than you cry?"

It's not part of a relationship to always bicker, fight and dislike one another. Sometimes, you go through depression from losing a job, loved one or dealing with an issue life presents us. It's okay to have disagreements but understand there is no such thing as a healthy toxic relationship. You may have seen television shows where both parties seemingly love to hate one another but I would be fearful of accepting that to be an honest truth. At least not a truth I'm willing to believe in. You know when your tears outweigh your moments of cheer. It's neither algebra nor trigonometry; it's addition and subtraction.

When you are in an exclusive relationship, especially in the first year, there will be many times where you find yourself in disarray about your partner's beliefs or actions. That's okay. Why? Because you're just getting to know them and still understanding the person you've incorporated in your life. In the same sense, it's not an excuse to endure more pain than pleasure. Inside of those moments of justified argument, have faith that it's temporary and rare in comparison to the peacetime. There's a story in *Think Rich Grow Rich* of a man who owned a gold mine. After finding gold, he went awhile without finding any gold. He eventually sold the mine to another man. Not long after owning the mine, the new owner found the largest depository of gold at the time. Sometimes we allow moments of unhappiness or uncertainty to determine the future of our relationship and that's not healthy. It's not about short moments but the overall equation.

When you look at your life, you should own little regrets. Some are gained when you were what we in the U.S. call, "Young and dumb" so they are excused. Others are from times when you weren't strong or wise enough to defend your actions. Lastly, there may have been instances when you made a life choice in lust or greed. As we age, the regrets lessen. Don't make having faith in keeping your relationship be that regret. All good relationships should have bad moments; it's what makes them great. Without them, we are preparing for a walking lie.

Some people keep from exploding, showing their true feeling or even hiding their emotions to keep from losing the other. it is there where you should find concern. One day, they or you will open up. When you do, if it took too long, it will appear exotically eccentric or evil. Why? Because you refrained from being honest with your feelings and behavior when you were justified in such expression. It's a mark of an adult to discern what the required and worthy action is for an issue. Similarly, it's imperative in such an occasion to release that action without fear of losing the person. Why? Because when you do it too late, it may be the reason they have faith that leaving you...won't be a regret.

Chapter 13:
FEP-C_®
Environmental Control

Chapter 13

F<u>E</u>P-C_®
Environmental Control

Who wears a bikini in the snow? Probably a "crazy" person, right? Definitely someone you wouldn't want to immerse your heart, time or health around for fear they might injure it. Well, that's how this portion of the formula works. You are in control of the environment you own. Please don't take this as giving you the ability to change the weather but you have just the same amount of influence as the weather does.

Most men tailor their actions around the women they're interested in. If men are used to dating women who allow vulgar language, drug usage and unchecked acts of aggression, this gentleman will be in his rights to keep up what has worked for him. It's human nature for men. We only do what works and that's the bottom line. If it didn't work with the other women, we would alter our actions but they permitted it, thus he found no wrong in halting his actions. No matter the past of this man, you owe it to yourself to demand how your environment is treated.

If you allow a man to use profanity around you, then you should be the first to cuss and applaud his usage of such language. If you like men who smoke, then you should light one up when he does, before he does or mention it as an activity. If you like men who enjoy sex more so than casual conversation, then every time he begins to converse about something, insert your intent to meet him with sex as a period to his conversation. Believe me, this will stimulate him to keep up all these actions because you own the right to push this mindset if you desire to indulge those actions. In the same sense, you also can end these proceedings by simply denying them in YOUR environment.

Have you noticed as you approach a yellow light, you slow down? How about when you see a speed limit sign, you tend to stay at or around that limit? Well, if not then, have you ever seen how focused you become to your driving technicalities when you see a police car or hear a siren? For some of us these are all too familiar actions courtesy of one too many tickets but for most, this makes sense. This relates to how you too can set an environment to cause a man to do only what you allow. In the very least, have him ultra cautious of your response to an inaccurate behavior in your environment.

One great example of this is domestic abuse. Many women, who are abused, if not all, don't enjoy this abuse. These women aren't insane or idiots. The common understanding or excuse for this is, "She must like it That's why she stays". No, it's not true, for most instances. These women didn't meet him as violent men. This man didn't introduce himself with a left hook and give her his number via tattooing it in her mind with abusive words. No, this man was probably polite, honest and everything she could ever imagine in a mate. Oddly and yet traditionally, he was met with a button or trial he couldn't overcome without acting justly or he used his degree of understanding which was to abuse. It all started at one area and met an extreme.

He either started to yell, push or belittle her in some fashion as a perverted preparation for an ugly action he was eventually planning to exercise. It was here where she could have changed her environment if she didn't meet the ultimate extreme...death.

Most intimate partner homicides occur between spouses, though boyfriends/girlfriends have committed about the same number of homicides in recent years. -Bureau of Justice Statistics, Intimate Partner Violence in the U.S. 1993-2004, 2006.

Many women attempt to adjust their environment but seldom do so with success due to the amazing heaviness of domestic abuse and its insatiable ability to insert compromise upon the abused. You don't want to say much because you could lose them and all the grand treatment they donate to your life but if you don't, you will eventually lose it all and maybe your life. It's the '**How**' where many are lost in changing this epidemic yet the '**Why**' is an underlying theme we ignore. Changing your environment in regards to domestic abuse isn't easy but necessary. If it doesn't cost you your life, it will be found in your health or pockets.

➤ The health-related costs of intimate partner violence exceed $5.8 billion each year. Of that amount, nearly $4.1 billion are for direct medical and mental health care services, and nearly $1.8 billion are for the indirect costs of lost productivity or wages. - Centers for Disease Control and Prevention, Costs of Intimate Partner Violence Against Women in the United States, April 2003.

➤ On average, more than three women and one man are murdered by their intimate partners in this country every day. . (Bureau of Justice Statistics Crime Data Brief, Intimate Partner Violence, 1993-2001, February 2003. Bureau of Justice Statistics, Intimate Partner Violence in the U.S. 1993-2004, 2006.)

➤ In 2000, 1,247 women were killed by an intimate partner. The same year, 440 men were killed by an intimate partner. Intimate partner homicides accounted for 30% of the murders of women and 5% percent of the murders of men. (Bureau of Justice Statistics Crime Data Brief, Intimate Partner Violence, 1993-2001, February 2003. Bureau of Justice Statistics, Intimate Partner Violence in the U.S. 1993-2004, 2006.)

If you take 3 deep 3-second breaths, when you finally exhale, one woman would have been killed, assaulted or beaten in the U.S. These women, who are abused, leave behind broken family relationships, ruined careers or a life of regretting enduring a horrific relationship for the sake of children who would enjoy no benefit of seeing their mother brutalized or murdered in their eyes. It may seem that I'm taking this to heart as I've proved my point but I'm a victim of domestic violence. I've been abused by a woman and watched a majority of women in my life be abused by men. They changed their environments and now don't indulge such treatment. I watched their **How** and studied my own **How** only to write this for you so you will know **How** to change your environment for the sake of your livelihood.

The most important part of your **How** lies in what you create as your environment and **How** imperative it is for you to keep such as such. When we delve into the chapter of conviction, you will have a fully functional idea of this term but we will play with it for now. While watching this amazing but brutal movie titled, "Machine Gun Preacher", it brought about the most thrilling example of the **How**.

In this movie (without spoiling it) actor Gerard Butler plays a former convict turned preacher, Sam Childers. What makes this movie compelling is the environmental change his wife, Lynn Childers, played by Michelle Monaghan, applied to her life. You see it's not about him it's about her. She decided that in HER environment there would be no drugs or stripping. She gave up exotic dancing, drugs and sin for the pursuit of Christ in HER environment.

Sam wanted her to bend for the sake of money troubles but she refused because in HER environment, stripping, drugs and sin wouldn't get her closer to Christ. Now, this is an amazing story which I won't dare commit what I believe is as close to a sin as anything by detailing how the ending plays out, however her actions succeeded. Hence, he became a preacher courtesy of HER environment not allowing drugs to have a part in it. She didn't need to yell, scream or fight him; she just refused to allow any of it inside and he eventually followed suit. Now ...there is a movie about him.

Her movements aren't impossible to duplicate. She only had to say the most powerful word a woman can utter regarding HER environment..."No". When you don't want abuse in your life, don't accept it. Is it that simple? If you believe so, it will be. If the moment he screams, holds you too long or display any sign of potential violent/aggressive treatment, you stop it right there and say, "No". Remember the age old, D.A.R.E motto of "Say No to Drugs"? Well, it was laughable to those who wanted that money to other programs but it was a tremendous and grand technique, which helped me avoid drug usage as a teen. The word "No" is beyond beautiful and causes immediate attention to whomever it's used upon. It's a magical weapon used to create peace. As Gandhi and Dr. King Jr. effectively used it.

It doesn't take much effort. If you believe in why you want your environment to be without a certain item or action, then you must believe in it. This is the key in the mystery of "No". When you believe abuse is wrong, drugs are wrong or sin is wrong, you have every right to refute it. This is where your strength is derived. As long as your "No" is to halt something reasonable, then you will, with time, meet success.

If you are asking him to stop smoking because you don't want to end up like millions of people with lung cancer, you can refuse to kiss, talk to or be around him when he smokes. It's a sign of respect for him to avoid displeasing you and an awesome promotion of respect you're given for being consistent. In honesty, keep it realistic to your basic needs. You can't or shall I say, shouldn't desire things because you are just genuinely aggravated of him. Example: "I'm tired of the why you breathe. It's so annoying. Can you not breathe like that everyday??" In that extreme (for some, not so extreme) example, you may find a mate would rather deem this, "petty" rather than something to be a true need of change. Furthermore, be sure to evaluate their past prior to seeking to change such an aggravating or eventually disruptive behavior.

In many cases, if not all, we behave a certain way courtesy of our upbringing. Not to linger the point about violence, however men who as children witnessed their parents' domestic violence were twice as likely to abuse their own wives as sons of nonviolent parents. - http://domesticviolencestatistics.org. When you ask about his past, if this is part of it, be sure to make a mental note. Make that part of your environment that violence or the continuation of such acts won't be permitted. Even if he details cheating, gambling, thefts...etc are previous nings he's been accustomed to, just store it in the, "Pay attention and halt when seen" list. Remember, your "No" will be your victory cry.

A real life example of how environmental change donates edifying affects to men rests in my current relationship. My partner is a pharmacist out of highly decorated Emory Hospital. She graduated top of her class in both University of Miami and Mercer University. Now, this isn't to highlight my princess yet to set up how her environment and mine don't mix but while I'm amiss her environment, it's respected thoroughly.

My education is based in the arts, mainly. Since a youth, I was gifted in painting, drawing and sculpturing. From this, I grew to become an orator, actor and educator. The exotic nature of being an artist inspires my mind to resemble my living style. If you ever see my car or home, the word, "mess" is an understatement. Every idea I could come up with is acted upon, dealt with attention then discarded to a cave-like area where other grand ideas are hoarded. I am notoriously known for losing my wallet, keys and in many cases…money (Which one would think should be in my wallet) Time after time I've left food in the sink until it's grown children, unattended garbage has began to reanimate and dirty socks seems to get up and leave due to such abandonment. This is really odd being that I'm pretty clean, for the most part. My body, food and overall health of mind aren't reflective completely of how I live. This is how I've been able to make life, as an awkward version of a nomadic minded adult. My princess doesn't share my attitude in any way shape or form. One couldn't, being that her profession is tied to cleanliness and organization. The opposite could mean the difference between life and death or lawsuit and career.

Everyday her bed is made up to perfection, something I rarely do. She rarely leaves dishes overnight, something I thought was an improvement on my end. She even has hand soap AND dish detergent. To all the men who aren't too tidy, that last statement brought about a unanimous "WHAT? Two Soaps? Why not use the dish soap for your hands too?" This is how I think. This is where our two environments meet respect and stay relatively unchanged, unless for the better.

As I visit her, I realized this is her home and not mine. Respect. Her dishes aren't mine. Respect. Her bed isn't mine. Respect. Thus, when it comes to respecting her, I didn't think it flowed to ruin her environment for the sake of my laziness. She mentioned a few times, "Please make my bed, untidiness bothers me". For someone you love, you will oblige such a simple task. Long story short, just by her "checking" me each time I left dishes unwashed, a bed unmade or didn't clean something, I realized that if I continued, I was in direct violation of the golden rule. (Treat others how you would like to be treated) I respected her environment enough t roll with it. Now, I've made her bed almost 300 times and each time unique from the last. (My artistic nature) It wasn't much energy needed on her end. All that was required is her drawing the line in the sand, "In m environment, I don't allow a filthy home." It was all she needed to recite. Not all recitals are done with words. I had to also follow how she behaved It would have been different if she didn't want me to dirty things up yet meanwhile, she was just as disgusting.

You control your environment by what you accept. If he respects you, he will follow suit. If he doesn't, it's either he doesn't respect you or your environment may not be in need of his following. if I was clean and she was dirty but she wanted to keep her environment dirty, it would have been immature to find argument in me cleaning up her mess. Sometimes we enjoy finding comfort in wrong and even reason to do so. If someone brings something to your environment that betters it, it's okay. It's only unti what they bring destroys or negatively infects the lifestyle you've lived. It is then when you will accept their disrespecting of your environment and endure the constant aggravation or modify your environment to set a compromise with theirs while they are around you. (Ex: Don't make bed but clean dishes) or realize disrespect isn't what you deserve then act accordingly.

Chapter 14:
FEP-C®
Penalty / Prize

Chapter 14

FEP-C®
Penalty/Prize

A man's ultimate lifelong reward for pleasing his woman is...her heart. In contrast, his ultimate penalty for displeasing her is...permanent eviction from her heart. Believe it or not, men are bred and led to treat you how we believe you desire to be treated. Yes, those men who ask for sex within the first 30 seconds of knowing you or are seemingly disrespected when you decline them for touching your body are...acting out of success. They were met with victory by using such tactics and without much penalty. This is how you can use a man's innate ability against him.

We learn from two things: failure and success. That's it. There is no magic or secret. Although it may seem as if I'm oversimplifying the effort needed, it's definitely the easiest portion of the formula. It is here where you can make the procedure enjoyable for yourself. In essence, it becomes a game. Something you actually can smile and find room to laugh at the results of your efforts. In the beginning, penalizing him for inappropriate actions and praising him for positive actions may seem difficult as well as childish but in retrospect...isn't that what brought you to be what you are now?

What happens when you get straight A's, for many a scholarship or reward. Well, let's amp that up. If you eat right, workout regularly and restrict stress, don't you benefit via better health? Hmmm...driving the speed limit keeps your insurance low and saves you hundreds of dollars in fines or lawyer fees. Well, the opposite of good grades would be bad grades which means no advanced education. Horrible lifestyle habits equals ruined skin then hastened life expiration. The same goes for speeding, which can equate to financial hardships, suspension of your license or even death. We learn what to do by the consequences associated with our actions. You can do the same to your mate with very similar results. Let's start with penalty.

We can begin with a few scenarios and actions. Example: First, if you want him to stop yelling, make sure you are prepared to penalize him for his yelling. Second, don't give him what he's asking for while committing the undesired act. Finally, detail why you aren't complying with his desires during the aftermath of his yelling. Now, here's a real world scenario on how you can apply the above between Bob and Shirley.

Bob: I hate when you invite your friends to everything we do!! Can' we have any time to ourselves??!

Shirley: ...(Silence):: Texting in her phone::

Bob: Can't you hear me?! Am I talking to my freaking self over here?!

Shirley: ...(Silence)::Continues texting::

Bob: Oh, you are texting them while ignoring me?! How childish, Shirl! (Hears his phone alert) ::Acknowledges his phone and goes toward it::

Shirley: ...(Silent) ::Waiting for Bob::

Bob: ...(Reads text aloud) "I've told you screaming isn't respectful and something I don't appreciate it. I have no problem discussing this issue with you after you've calmed down or decided to speak without yelling. Please, make a choice because I care for your concerns but won't stoop to barking at one another when disagreements arise. –Shirl"
::Bob calms down and speaks to Shirley::
Sweetheart, you're right. We aren't children and should handle ourselves with more discipline. Although this situation irks me, as a man, I should lead by example and refrain from expressing myself through anger or outbursts. Can we talk about this over dinner? My treat.

Shirley: (Smiling) Yes, we can.

To some, they would like to think this isn't realistic. Rather deeming the scenario "fairytale like". If you are one of those who may have such a mindset think about this, can you go through drive thru...without a car? While some have tried, the technology of today won't allow a person to walk through a drive-thru nor will the employees of such a business. Take this into account, whatever you accept, a man will do. If you accept his yelling he will amplify or maintain his undesired action. It's plain and simple. Imagine if they allowed people to walk through drive-thrus. Who would wait inside when they could jog by, get their order and jog off? As a matter of fact, then why would they name it, "drive-thru"? Wouldn't that be a contradiction? It would cause disruption, confusion and chaos all courtesy of an organization not keeping order or consistency with their instructions to build a grand business.

Now, you are the business. In order for it to work customers can't believe your warnings or directions are negotiable. They should see you follow them and won't bend for the sake of a rebellious customer who

94

wants to walk through a drive through. If you start this trend now, the customer won't respect the business nor will the employees or passerby. Why? Because if you can't penalize someone for doing what you deemed disrespectful then you've just donated a reason for them not to respect you...since you don't respect yourself enough to keep your standards. There should be a penalty.

No man should disregard your standards and exchange his disregard with disrespect of your standards. Acceptance of the above is what toxic and poisonous relationships are riddled with. You can't allow disrespect to be commonplace in your relationship. It's what separates the single, miserable and broken women from those who are in happy, healthy and magical relationships. If he yells, you stay silent and reintroduce your, "No yelling" policy. If he cheats, you don't have sex with him, give him any attention or refuse his gifts for six months. If he abuses you verbally, physically or spiritually, you tell him, "I don't appreciate nor deserve this treatment". If you must, leave, call the police or inform his family or close friends who aren't familiar with this behavior. The previous are all a few examples and are to be used if he disrespects your standards. Whatever the penalty, make sure it's justifiable for the act. You set it but enforce it. One important aspect of the penalty is making sure at the end of the penalty is a prize.

As our character Shirley found success in Bob treating her to a meal and lowering his voice, Shirley could have wrote Bob a note stating, "Thank you for respecting me". Such a small gesture goes a long way to men. Women mistake us at times. Either they're given horrible advice from other women or misguided men with hidden agendas. Many times men are portrayed as insensitive, cantankerous and impervious to nonsexual romance. None can be untrue about our gender.

We enjoy smiling, laughing and being given gifts for our deeds. It's the twisted version of this mindset that has caused turmoil for many women. Instead of applauding him for doing right, some men are ignored for the good they do and jeered for their bad behavior or...praised for it.

Men are dubbed, "soft, lame or square" if they tell their mate, "Gifts for my good deeds make me smile". Your goal in any relationship is to create an atmosphere where who and what you are isn't shunned because of your belief system. Many good men hide behind a false veil of toughness to slowly ease their princess into who he really is. He was afraid to say, "I like walking, painting or writing short stories to clear my mind". A man who's in touch with his inner self and can articulate how he deserves

95

to be treated or loved in addition to loving you the way you should isn't always seen as, "believable".

I've even grown weary of how the term, "too good to be true" has become common for a man who respects your wishes and treats you wit honor. Rubbish!

God has made an earth filled with men who are "too good to be true" but you should believe you deserve "too good to be true" instead o "just harmful enough to be realistic". Good men who seem too amazing to be human are in all cities. These are the men who should be given a prize. Even if he's lying, at least allow FAKING to be good to win over being evidently horrible. Bad boys don't have to fake being good, their effortless badness is enough. If a man lies about being good but still treats you like a queen, then so be it. At least you didn't lose much in comparison to the woman who endures a terrible relationship with an evil man who handled her brutally. Even if both women shared an equal amount of time, the brutalized woman will still covet being lied to instead of living with demonic truth.

I'm not sponsoring lying or promoting nor encouraging men to lie. This idea is only to inspire women towards prizing men for their positive actions. It's something we utterly enjoy but don't receive enough. It's how we learn what you like, love and hate.

Even during intimacy, how do you think we figure out your kissing technique? If you start to shy away from kissing us, we will conjure the thought, "Maybe I'm doing something wrong". In the same token, if you initiate kissing, we will think, "I must be doing something right". It's all in the prize. A prize can be a smile, kiss, thank you, note, gift or word.

Your prize is what builds a man to be a better man. It's what softens us to realize there is fruit in being good. Understand men have figured women out to an ugly degree. This understanding is hurtfully true to an extent but dangerous to our collective futures.

We've learned being mean to you will still get us attention, hence the "Bad Boy" section. We know, as long as we play along with what society deems as, "desirable" we will win the prize of...your heart.

Some hearts have grown rotten because of how many men have played the bad boy role, injured a woman and thus motivated her interest in women, promiscuity or suicide. All of these bad boys were brought to believe being bad produced good prizes. If it were untrue, vhy would they indulge in this behavior? If no woman slept with a "bad boy" then there would be no bad boys...on earth. Remember, women have the ultimate control of what type of man is produced in this world based on whom they entertain. Women could say today, "Men who ride bicycles and wear bicycle shorts are sexy" by this time tomorrow...Huffy and Nike would be trillion dollar companies then Lance Armstrong would be considered a human god (pre-confession). It's all in what you give prize to. You can build what you need by what you indirectly use to destroy what you need.

"A woman should soften but not weaken a man"-Sigmund Freud. This best illustrates why prize is important. It creates in us a sign of hope. Hope realized in our childhood yet distorted in our adult years then deemed, "unrealistic". What am I referring to? The hope of the goodness in man. What a beautiful world it would be if being good were the only way to receive attention, love or prize. Do you realize most of the U.S. news broadcasts are of "bad news" no matter the subject? The President can sign a bill to give everyone free food for life and it costs no one anything. There would be little news about how it helps the country and more broadcasts on he must be the devil to conjure up something so perfect...it has to be sinister. You have a choice: Follow the world or give him prize for doing "good". Even if miniscule or something he's supposed to do. It has to start somewhere. Wherever it starts, it softens the hardness the world built into us and brings us to realize the glory in goodness.

Bob: Sweetheart, I know you were going to be late so I tried...tried to make you dinner but burnt everything edible. So instead, I made cereal because I've had more practice and knew I wouldn't mess that up.

Shirley: Babe, you are a sweetheart. You know, I normally don't eat cereal for dinner but since you made it...I'll make an exception. My little Cereal Chef! Now, promise me you'll tell me your secret to make great cereal and give me three kisses if I eat it.

(They laugh)

Bob: I promise. Now eat it before it gets soggy and becomes soup cereal.

It was a simple gesture of appreciation but *guarantee you me** he is reading up on exotic ways to make cereal or other dishes just for those three kisses. You can bet from now on, he will relish in times when she

97

comes home late. Prize: a simple word but a powerful avenue in inspiring your mate to know what makes you happy.

No matter the case always end each penalty with a prize otherwise you may run the risk of inserting prolonged depression in a relationship. Once they've gained an understanding of their wrong, apologized (if needed) or agreed to disagree, move on and set focus to constructing a positive relationship. What you penalize and what you give prize for is how your happiness will be built.

*= Guarantee you me: Southern colloquialism meaning, "believe me"

Chapter 15:
FEP-C̲®
Conviction

Chapter 15:

FEP-C®

Conviction

If you lie to others and convince them of your lie, you're a genius. If you lie to yourself and convince yourself of your lie, you are a genius. If you lie to others but don't convince yourself of this lie, the others will find out and find the stupidity in your lie and call you…a liar. What do you call a man who doesn't play basketball, can't dribble, never stepped on a court but calls himself a "Professional Basketball Player"? You call him a liar. Until you put a ball in his hand and challenge his truth, you may call him a "Professional Basketball Player" too. In this chapter, I want you to realize lying to yourself about what you deserve and won't accept will become your undoing. You may not be called a liar but you will be treated as one. If not by your mate, then definitely to yourself.

Have you ever heard of someone trusting a liar? It's almost a contradiction but in reality, that's what you would have to do to love a liar. You would have to exist in a contradiction. You can't trust what they say, where they are or what they're doing but you do only to run into a lie that bites your ears for trusting what you were listening to. When it comes to conviction, either you better become the best liar in the world or honestly love yourself enough to say, "This is what I want, because I deserve and will accept nothing less". Conviction is the last remaining portion of "Changing Him".

Without conviction in your demands, it's like expecting someone to stop speeding by informing them, "If you speed again, I won't give you a ticket, but I may pull you over and tell you not to speed again." Many of our drivers with horrible records would enjoy having an officer state the above rather than another ticket plus 4 -8 hours of driving school. In this case, you would only succeed by being the strict officer. Would you respect the law if all officers let you off each and every time you broke the law? Odds are, many of us wouldn't. Most barely respect fully enforced laws, imagine if they were in the environment of unendorsed laws. This world would be in disarray, right? Well, this is how many of the issues in male to female connection have gone eerily wrong.

Any woman can say, "I deserve a man who opens doors every time, doesn't yell and respects me." That is a beautiful and eloquently stated sentence, however if she runs into a man who doesn't open doors, cusses her out in public and disrespects her daily, that "eloquence" is just as viable as a degree you can get...from a gas station. The difference between a wife and "booty call" is conviction. Point blank.

Conviction is a simple term and can determine where you are in his phone, heart or mind. Most men will marry a woman who has utterly unbreakable dignity and that's found in her conviction. She can talk all day about being a princess but if her actions don't match, then he will see her as less than the princesses' maid . When you know you aren't saying, " I deserve a man who opens doors" as topic of discussion but as a true, unbendable and unconditional expectation, then you will treat it as such. Say what you mean and mean what you say isn't the end of the phrase. Say what you mean, mean what you say and match what you're saying to your actions. Now that encompasses conviction.

Making this work in a relationship isn't difficult but it's actually something you've been doing since birth. Example: When a baby is hungry, he or she will cry until they're fed. The parents could give the baby its favorite toy, a clean diaper and a bath...that baby would still cry. It was conviction at its best. The baby made the parents move. They found food, the baby stopped crying and now they can live free without tears crowding their ears. How is a baby able to do what many aren't? Solely because we fear losing someone so much that we are willing to lose ourselves to keep them. Belief in this motto is what allows us to lose them.

A woman who lives in conviction is more attractive than an awesome mixture of Halle Berry, Lucy Liu, Julia Roberts, Angela Basset and Jennifer Lopez. Why, because a woman with conviction is trustworthy, consistent and loyal. These three traits outweigh beauty and defeat it 10/10 times. It starts and ends with what you believe in.

What you believe in is what you believe in. If you can't see fault in it, then keep believing in it. Men respect women who refuse to lose hope in their beliefs. If you were raised to go to church weekly, then do so. If he doesn't believe in going to church, that has no bearing on your attendance. However, the moment you stay at home and commence to follow his belief, he will question why you ever cared about it in the first place. If you made a point to say, "In my relationship, I must have a partner who loves God enough to visit church weekly" yet he never bent and you did, well you just lost a point on the Integrity Board. Think about that baby. All the baby did was stick to their guns and the parents made note, refused to submit then submitted. It can work for any mate as well, as long as you believe in what you believe in.

It's in your actions, not your words. Your words are like the gas to a car but without you pushing the pedal, the vehicle is going nowhere and no one will believe it works. If you want a man to open doors, the process simple but the conviction is what separates your talk from your walk. Let's explore the door scenario.

You mention, "I believe a respectable lady shouldn't open doors. Opening doors is a sign of a man desiring to relieve momentary stress from his mate. Although I can do it myself, it's a simple sign that he knows I have arms but would rather me not use the energy from them for a moment." Now, as they approach the car door, she stands outside of it and he opens the door. Typical. Most men who respect you will do that. As you encroach upon your destination, the "moment" presents itself. This is where most women fail. The man will get out of the car and so will the woman. Her excuse can be, "I forgot" or "I'm not used to a man opening doors." Whatever she says, she just lost another Integrity point. Instead of getting out, she should have sat and waited. A man would rather bend than lose face. He just listened to you suggest that opening doors are a form of flattery and respect. If he objects, he's definitely telling you about your worth. You sit in that car and don't touch that door. He will open that door. Once he opens the door, then you wait for him to open the door to the place of business you two are entering. IF FOR ANY MOMENT YOU BELIEVE THIS IS A WASTE OF YOUR TIME, YOU HAVE BECOME PART OF THE REASON WHY MEN FEEL AS IF WORKING FOR YOU IS POINTLESS. THIS SIMPLE GESTURE IS A LOST ART BUT SHOULD NOT BE.

You deserve "earnership". In essence, you deserve to be earned and conviction is the admission fee of entry into your heart. Conviction is consistency of your beliefs. If you don't believe in eating poison, no matter my actions, I guarantee you nothing will entice you to eat poison. You would fight tooth and nail to refute my efforts but you wouldn't eat the poison. When a man meets a woman who stands by her beliefs, it inspires him to respect her. This man will either date, marry you or place you on the "shelf".

The shelf is where many good women are placed when a man isn't ready to give up his "chase". As a man ages, we start to recognize the goodness of certain women, much of which is deciphered through their convictions. If she's rarely seen in scanty attire, under the influence and refuses to discuss sexual desires with the gentleman she may be shelved. If he's not in the mindset to date her, he will place her in the back of his mind (shelf) as, "Wife" material. This is a very clever and typical of a man. Is our way of singling out women who will allow us to gain them for a discounted price or free versus full price. When ready, he will come back to his shelf and if you're the best out of those whom are left, he will all of a sudden resume conversations even years later. If you aren't one of the following, he will poke around at potentially rekindling the relationship:

1. Pregnant by a man who isn't aimed at being more than a sperm donor (also affectionately deemed "loser, deadbeat or waste of space") Thus inspiring bitterness in your attitude. It's not so much the child, but the resulting damage by the deadbeat. All men like women with less baggage.

2. Out of shape (as women tend to lose the energy to keep in shape over the years) Good health inspires longevity of life and reproduction. All men like attractive women.

3. Visually depressed by the landscape of your life. A smile before he meets you means you will smile more when he does. All men like happy women.

Being shelved is actually what many men do subconsciously. When we aren't ready, we rather keep you in arms reach to give you situational attention until we're ready to give you what you deserve. This will ONLY occur if we know you're worth it, which is all based on your conviction level. The worst disease many women are infected with is, Negotiable Standards Disease (NSD).

NSD is a horrible infection in homes, hearts and minds all across America. In reality, many women are seemingly fearful of adding conviction with their standards. Never realizing a lack of consistency in your conviction inspires us to be...lesser men. We don't have a reason to live as a personable great man when being an unpleasant mediocre man meets your standards. It's your ability to challenge us, which compels us to love better, live better and lead better. However, if being an 'okay' man were all we need to be, then why would we run the risk of being a good man and scaring you away? When you challenge us toward greatness, we in turn will push you. *"It takes a good woman to bring out the best in a man. It takes a good man to bring out the best in a woman." -***Honorable Louis Farrakhan.** The consistency of your conviction is what we pay attention to and how we build an idea of you being what you say you are.

Consistency of conviction. If you tell him "I don't touch doors. Every man I date opens my door. If not, I don't go in or get out of the car or building." Yet when he forgets a couple times...so do you. He will realize that you weren't serious with your requests. He will know you just wanted to say that because it "sounds right". From there, he will play Double Dutch with your orders. The pure logic of training a human or any animal is consistency. If you punish a baby for spilling milk on the carpet today, but tomorrow when they do it again, you just clean it up without penalizing them, you just sent a mixed signal, "Maybe mommy doesn't mind me doing that". The same concept goes for men. When mixed messages are sent, he will repeat his actions. From time to time, he will do the right things just to appease you, all the while never changing because he knows..."she really doesn't care about this. She's just confused".

You owe it to yourself to demand what you deserve with an unrelenting mindset. It won't scare us away, make us dislike you or intimidate us. Honestly, if not for the awesome women who provoked my efforts, I wouldn't have the accolades I've accumulated thus far. I have more awards in 9 years than most receive in a lifetime. My entire house is decorated in awards. Each award has a story. All stories are connected to a woman who I dated, who supported me or loved me into being a better man. Something I saw in their makeup, mindset or words gave me an unbelievable urge to better myself. Now there is no turning back because I'm convinced every woman wants to be treated the way they deserve, only if they refuse any other form of treatment.

One woman in particular did something unbelievably new to me. I was 20 at the time she was 21. This woman at the time was my greatest adult girlfriend. Out of the 5 I've cared for, she is still #2. What made her amazing was her...conviction, you guessed it. She earned a 3.8 Grade Point Average, spoke 5 different languages, never kissed a man, no boyfriend and a virgin. When we spoke, no conversations of sex were permitted. It wasn't just her refusing but never initiating any topic aimed in a sexual direction. I was her first kiss and boyfriend but in order for me to become such, I took a month of no communication with any other woman to "purify" myself for her. In the end, it was her ability to believe in her Christian beliefs, which lead her to not want sex before marriage and not bend because I was an attractive, smart, sweet-talking and persistent American. Her, "No" was more powerful than any woman's "Yes". She meant what she said and said what she meant. This was the reason why today, I open doors, respect women and fight to inspire women to know...every man can love you like I do or more if you challenge us to. You are our example of sensitive, care and love.

The woman is our first nurse. You taught us why it's okay to cry. We came to you when we felt weak and needed strength. Now, you still are.

You are why we sing songs, act tough and make jokes during sad scenes of love movies. Have you ever noticed in every "Gangsta" rap song, there is always a mention of a woman? No matter if it's a derogatory term, or if she's in the hook or actually rapping, women are topic of discussion, even momentarily. Most can't write a song without you being a motivation. It's what you believe in which directs us on how to love you better or worse. If you don't accept something, don't bend to keep us because you will lose us. That's not an accidental repeat. Whatever you don't accept, don't accept it until death. You will never lose when fighting to keep your integrity. Real men love integrity, boys fear it. If you have many men fearful of your stances on sex, chivalry or relationship statuses...then you may find yourself scaring boys who shouldn't be in your life to begin with. You are our everything and the worse thing you can do...is not holding us accountable for treating you the way you deserve.

In my last book "Love Is Not An STD", I wrote, "Most women deserve to F.I.S.L.E". F.I.S.L.E is what I call the basic building block of love. Without a foundation, it's bound to crumble, as many do. F.I.S.L.E breaks down into Faith, Inspiration, Support, Leadership and Education. If you believe you deserve someone who cares for their religious beliefs in addition to help build yours, is willing to inspire you, one who can support you with words or actions in times of need, a co-leader in the relationship, not dictator or follower and someone who can educate you about things you've never before known courtesy of conversations or lessons, then you want to "F.I.S.L.E". This isn't hard but necessary to be loved. Anyone who cares enough to make you F.I.S.L.E cares enough to do so because of your conviction. When a man sees you aren't a "talker" but a woman who's words, actions and beliefs all match, then you will F.I.S.L.E. Not only that, you will also meet love in a way you wouldn't have if you submit to being everything he wants you to be which include nothing you deserve to be. Conviction is the key.

*Earnership =to be earned by your standards.

106

Chapter 16:
FEP-C® In Motion

Chapter 16:

FEP-C$_®$ In Motion

Below are example stories putting FEP-C ® in a real life scenario. Although I've taken the names off these essays, many of them are based on true stories.

Temporary Married to a Mistake

She met him at the gym. As he approached, she smiled. Cute words, charm and a few laughs later, she gave up her number. He only called at awkward times because he works quirky hours. He mostly texts because of his "job" requirements. They meet up for dinner. She's infatuated with her inability to obtain all his attention. This man has her in a fairytale land. Everything he says makes her blush. His words are like poems. They have much fun together. They dream together. They have sex together. Some of him is missing so she investigates why she can't have more. After denying her intuition about there being something wrong with this "perfect" man, she finally becomes the detective. She digs.

He's married. He has children. He lives with his wife. She confronts him. He denies. She interrogates. He denies. She pesters. He denies. She shows investigative proof…he admits. His excuse, a traditional one: "I'm in an unhappy marriage. We are getting a divorce. I love you. I don't love her anymore. Just give me time. This will be over soon." He shows divorce paperwork. Time passes, they have more sex and nothing changes. *She buys this book.* She ponders, "If I can get him to fully commit to me, I will be happy." She believes in him being the man she needs, begins to believe his words and the mention of them working it out.

She has **faith** all will work out. They pray together, plan a future and continue to have sex. Around her, she doesn't allow him to call his children or wife. This is her **environmental control**. He obliges. Whenever he doesn't call, arrive at the hotel or her house on the time he says, she **penalizes** him by refusing sex. It angers him. When he makes calls and visits on time, she gives him sex as a **prize**. Exhausted of this seemingly forever noncommittal relationship, she makes her ultimatum, "Either me or her."

She makes this demand with sheer **conviction** refusing to wait any longer for exclusive love from the lover she loves. He doesn't bend, attempts to prolong the sexual relationship but she doesn't bend. He lies. Shows signed documents and changes phones to prove it's over. She believes, doubts and digs. He was lying...

She finds out by visiting his home only to see him happily with his wife. Later that night she compiles pictures and video of what she noted. She confronts him only to be told, "Don't you get it?! You're just a mistress You are for sex. It's a fantasy. I love her, I only lust you. Never come by my home, my wife and family or I'll call the police. Get it together or get out of my life." She gets it. She's hurt. She fails at changing him.

Lesson: You can't change a man...that's not yours.

Just a Call

They met at a club. Exchanged numbers. Same night...sex night. He didn't call the next day. She noticed. He calls the next week. She rushes to the phone. He's charming. He's funny. He's flirtatious. She's happy. She wants more. She gets an address. She arrives without panties, as he suggests. They have sex again. Passionate. Timeless. Mesmerizing.

He leaves first. She stays. Thinks about the beauty of the moment. He repeats this the next week. Instead of calls, she gets a text. She notices, but doesn't provoke argument. He repeats the invite another week later. She comes. She lies down. She enjoys this moment. He leaves first again. He only texts. Seemingly only invites her out at night. The movies, meals and occasional bowling. Nothing where many people are present. Rarely during the day. She catches on. Asks him, "the question." She says, "What are we?" He replies, "Cool." Befuddled she refuses to dig deeper, accepts the response and they meet up again for sex.

Time passes and the repetition becomes normal. Text, invite and sex. *She buys this book.* Wanting to find a way to become more than, "cool." She invited him to church. Believing that **faith** will show him a different side of her. He doesn't come. She has **faith** that he will. He complies. Arrives. Leaves. Then repeats their original cycle. She adapts to having him call instead of texting. Her **environmental control** regarding her time. In her world, she doesn't only communicate via text. He submits. Sparse conversations. Short words. When he texts for sex, she doesn't respond. Her **penalty** for texting is no sex. When he calls, charms and nvites, she gives him the **prize** between her legs for his obliging. She is consistent in this routine.

She follows it with **conviction**. He stops calling. Stops texting. Stops nviting. She invites him to church. Texts. Calls. Only runs into silence. He eventually responds, "You're too much. We're just cool and you are making all these demands. I have stuff to do. Can't bother with a chick who doesn't know her place. If you were my girlfriend, yeah, but you can't make these demands and be so burdensome when you're just a booty call. Please stop calling, texting and bothering me." She realizes a man's heart isn't found through his penis. If you start a relationship on just sex, that's what it will almost always end in. If there wasn't conversation about goals, life, love...etc, then you're just someone he's attracted to. Love is not an STD and giving your body as a form of love currency is failure waiting to happen. She read it, She's hurt. She fails at changing him.

Lesson: If you're just a booty call, you don't hold any place in a man's heart. Only women in his heart can change him.

Flawed Goods

After class he approached. Handsome, courteous and persistent. She gave her number. They spoke daily. Met up for coffee, smoothies and lunch often. It was a great friendship building. He was there to help. She was there to support. They went to church together. **Faith** is important to them. They had **faith** that making **faith** part of their requirements would benefit them. He asked her to be his girlfriend. She agreed. They became intimate after he said, "I love you." It was her standard to only have sex with men who are her boyfriends and are in love with. It was a word she lived in with **conviction**.

During the beginning stages of their relationship, he had a bad day and during an argument, he cussed at her. She was lost for words. Never being cusses to. It hurt. *She bought this book.* She had **faith** such was just an accident due to the bad day. However, she knew to not allow it to go unnoticed so it would be seen as, "acceptable." She didn't believe in allowing it to slip so, she made sure that her ***environmental control*** was that no man cussed around her no matter the circumstances. When other arguments arose and he would lash out with another cuss words, she would ignore him for a week. It was her **penalty**. When he would argue without cussing, when it was over, she would kiss him or buy him his favorite ice cream, it was her **prize.** She kept her actions consistent. She did it with **conviction**, now she doesn't have to worry about this issue anymore. Now onto changing other issues that may arise. She changed him.

Lesson: Any man who loves you, cares for you and wants you to know he does, won't mind changing for you. Especially when he knows it was wrong.

Chapter 17:
Egypt's "Shoulds"

gypt's "Shoulds"

While you now know how to "Change Him" understand in every relationship, there are a multitude of things that **should** occur. When it comes to changing a man, some women aren't aware of things they can change. Sometimes, you may be in a place where you don't need or want any change. That's grand! Instead, your relationship may need a little spice for you both, instead of changing him. These are changes you two **should** accomplish together.

If any of these "shoulds" are things you would enjoy having in your relationship, add them.
Below are a few "shoulds".

➢ **Pray together**

o Without God in your relationship, you don't have a relationship. In the Holy Bible it states, "Unless the Lord builds the house, its builders labor in vain."(Psalm 127) If praying isn't a consistent part of your relationship, then make it so. There is nothing more powerful than two people who have God backing the cohesiveness of their relationship. If God's involved, you now have a sand castle made with stone. Let God be the rock in your foundation.

➢ **Working out together and eating healthier.**

o We live in a society where people own gym membership, gym attire and gym food… but rarely use them (maybe the gym attire). Taking care of your body is a beautiful and necessary task. If we can workout together, we can live longer together. Many couples waste many good years without keeping in shape. This helps lose attraction from their mate, self-esteem and an appetite for being sexy. Help each other stay sexy. When you add better choice meals to your lifestyle, this helps extend your life. Not only so, it also helps prevent costly visits to the hospital. Without good health, you pass by the doctor visit and go straight into the ER. Eating healthier voluntarily is better than courtesy of doctor's orders. It won't hurt. It can be hard. Yet, it will only help that love become legendarily long.

➢ Make it new...no matter how old

o Make opening doors, traveling, going dancing, body painting, mountain climbing, zip lining or sculpting...etc all part of new adventures. Keep attempting to impress each other. It's not impossible but all part of that legendarily long love. Take your time in kissing them, write love notes or sing horrible songs. Keep the relationship interesting by being as creative as possible. If you need help, go online, ask a friend or recreate an old idea with new additions. Make it new by challenging each other to create fresh exciting ways to love one another. You never know...might end up creating your own book from this exercise.

➢ Getting tested. (Blood Pressure, STD and Cholesterol)

o Many of us are walking ticking time bombs. We are moments away from a heart attack, aneurysms or having HIV slow down our day. Visit the clinic, health fair or doctor together. There is nothing more amazing than a couple that knows their health statuses. In America, where obesity, high blood pressure and other preventable health issues are on the rise, doing this will show your mate the longevity of this love matters.

➢ Read a book

o If they don't like the books you read and vice versa, good! Explore the idea of trying something new. When you read a book together you can understand your mate's mind and ways of behaving. You can understand why she loves romance novels or thrillers and why he can't put down suspense titles. No matter if it's a magazine or 500-page book, the goal is to read something together to grow together.

Chapter 18:
As I Leave...Remember

Set standards you believe in and won't change. He will have no choice but to respect and follow. ~ Egypt

Chapter 18:
As I Leave...Remember.

Please remember, this book is a testimony of my growth as a man. These messages and stories are real life scenarios and you can duplicate them. Hopefully only the positive and healthy portions.

As for now, as I conclude, understand you have the power to bring men back to God. Make sure your change ends with having you two pray more and go to church more. Without the woman, we have no reason to change. Be our reason.

Remember, change takes time. It's work. Your mate may mess up, it may become cumbersome, but don't expect an overnight success for negative behavior which took them years to perfect. Your patience will be your victory song or silent defeat.

This is history of how humans change, not just men. If women can urge this change in men, we then will see overall great people in love. It starts with where your heart is. He has to have a destination and goal to work towards.

In the end, the main goal is to lock your heart with God, inspire the man to reach God through your standards. From there he will get to your heart...through Him. When man finally comes back to loving the woman the way God does, many relationships won't end in such misery. The challenge is yours now. Change him.

The easiest man to change is a man who knows you're worth changing for. ~ Egypt

Biography of American Author "Egypt"

It's painful for anyone to lose a mother and watch their family slowly reduced to small gangs instead of one enormous unit. Imagine being a 12 year old. What's even more difficult is hearing your father tell you, "I don't want you boy" which added poisonous salt to an already infected broken heart. Eventually, you realize the life you live will never be what you knew. A 12 year old only left with memories of laughter, happiness and joy that will always remain vanishing images of what used to be. Tears, agony and depression set in...Again imagine being 12.

Classified as an orphan, despite having an 18 year old sister to care for him, Egypt rode the wave many young fatherless boys travel...crime. Brutally beating classmates, bullying, selling drugs, pimping, theft, getting arrested and vandalism were his methods of expression. He used these mediums as an outlet for the hurt this world impacted upon him. Yet, there was a saving grace.

Egypt's mother's dying wish was for him to become an artist. Gradually he began to utilize his artistic talent in painting and drawing to create his world. From such, he used that skill in all walks of his life. From joining the Stoneman Douglas High School Step Team alongside Francisco Hernandez, boxing with John Hirnyk, Henry Maya, Jason Maya and Jeff Poritz in addition to finding his African mind, Egypt ceased to hate the world what for it took from him and began to find ways to give back.

His sister, Chasity Robinson, besides God, is Chukia Williams, her daughter Diamond Bynes and son Kenrick Thomas, he realized love isn't about doing things for money, attention or to get a return; love is a donation. With this motivation and having his head on straight, Egypt transitioned to what many know of him now.

Over a span of 9 years Egypt has led a life many consider a fairytale. His work in Black history storytelling, relationship counseling and HIV education/performing has opened doors many seldom see. He's appeared on MTV, BET on 3 occasions, Apollo Theater twice, FOX with Lee Pitts in addition to countless radio, magazine and performance appearances. Egypt has shared stages with A-list celebrities such as John Legend, Alicia Keys and Magic Johnson. Even began friendships with millionaire businessman Arthur Wylie and actor Irone Singleton. He's touched stages in Johannesburg South Africa, Doha Qatar, Amman Jordan, Barbados, Trinidad and Tobago. Not to neglect he's earned two degrees while being on the Dean's list, graduating Phi Theta Kappa Honors, winning the 147lbs Florida State Boxing Championship, creating the AIDS Awareness Poets Inc, founding the AIDS Games and writing two top selling relationship books, "How Good Is Sex?" in addition to "Love Is Not An STD".

He is proof, that no matter how your life starts, you can change the middle and alter the ending. His story has inspired many and continues to be a reason why some believe their yesterday won't dictate their tomorrow because they've made a decision to live right...today. Ladies and gentleman, the incomparable...Devin T. Robinson X "Egypt"

122

Acknowledgements

My Sister Chasity, I love you and thank you for your sacrifice.

Mrs. Williams. Thank you for bringing my history to me.

My Little Sister Chukia, I love you. Be the mom you know you can be.

My Niece Diamond, I love you and don't entertain garbage men.

My Nephew Kenrick "Lil X" I love you and be the man you will be.

My Dad. Thanks for my amazing story. Your absence made me a man.

My Uncle Tom, I love you for being the man I wish to be.

Ruffins, Pop and mom, I thank God for giving me another set of parents.

Rodriguez's Family, Thank you for teaching me determination.

Hernandez's Family, Thank you for showing me family.

Stitts' family, Thank you for showing me faith.

Mariel, Thank you for supporting me before I was me.

Sevown, Thank you for giving me a place to stay in college.

Ancel, Thank you for being the leader I needed to see.

Randy, Thank you for donating time, energy and effort to my cause.

Ms. Robinson, Thank you for helping inspire my love for HIV education.

Christele, Thank you for being the best girlfriend I could dream of.

Jasmin McNeil, Thank for crying when you saw me on BET. Inspiration.

Duane Boucard, Thank you for not forgetting what friendship is.

Brian Poem, Thank you for being my road buddy.

Noel Stitt, Thank you for being the best friend money could buy, ha!

Francisco Hernandez, Thanks for being the best friend cash can't buy, ha!

Mable Dell Robinson Mother, I love you mommy and thank you for Chas.

Chrisnatha, Thanks for believing in me.

Venise and Gloria, Thank you for being the first to believe in me.

Irone Singleton, Thank you for being the example I needed to see.

All supporters, Thank you for never giving up on my dreams. Without you, I would be a man writing a letter to himself. You believe in my work and are the breath I breathe.

A Gift for YOU!
(for buying this book)

100 Ways To Make Them Smile

**Email "100" to YouCan@ChangeAMan.com
and receive a FREE copy of:**

*100 Ways To Make Them Smile**

* You only pay $3.50 for shipping